What people are saying about …

A CALL TO ACT

"Too often, Christians have used our faith as a ticket into heaven and a license to ignore the broken world we live in. We have promised a hurting world that there is life after death, while so many are wondering if there is life before death. In this book, Natalie and Martin invite you into a faith that is not just about going to heaven when you die, but bringing heaven to earth while you live. This is an invitation to join the revolution of Jesus. After all, Jesus did not come to help us escape the world; he came to help us transform this world. Read this manifesto of justice, and let the revolution begin inside of you. May your life be good news to the poor."

Shane Claiborne, Author, Speaker, Activist,
and Co-founder, Red Letter Christians

"A clear, timely, and prophetic call to the church to prioritise the poor in our society. This inspiring and practical book is a must-read for all Christians."

Gavin Calver, CEO, Evangelical Alliance

"Following God can never be separated from sharing his heart for the righting of injustice, the relief of suffering, or the end of poverty. As Martin and Natalie say, 'Isaiah calls it "True Fasting" and James calls it "True Religion"', but I am grateful to them both for reminding us all of what 'True Discipleship' means in practice."

Paul Harcourt, National Leader,
New Wine England

"Rock-face realities, Christian compassion, and biblical boldness combine to make this a compelling book. It will help develop our understanding and win our response to the demanding challenges being faced in our modern culture."

Terry Virgo, Founder, Newfrontiers

"The challenge at the heart of this book is to serve through proximity, to get close. Close enough to feel the dead weight in our lives of the stuff we consume and hoard. Close enough to see the negative impact of our choices on people we're called to love in Jesus' name.... Consumerism is a dull embrace of the life we're made for—this book will inspire you with a bright yet simple vision for following Jesus in complex times."

Rachel Gardner, Director of
National Work, Youthscape

"Christians love to talk about the bias to the poor, as long as it's just talk. All too often we fail to confront the cost of placing the poor at the centre, because we will only eradicate poverty when we are willing to make deep sacrifices and amend our own lifestyles. This prophetic book challenges us on the most personal level to be more Christ-like so that we can change our world. By making it clear that discipleship and a passion for justice are one and the same, Martin Charlesworth and Natalie Williams have given us a book to which all Christians need to attend and respond. If you're happy being complacent, don't go near it. If you're up for the deeper conversion necessary to transform your community under Christ, you must read it."

Philip North, Bishop of Burnley

"Newspapers still tell us church attendance is falling inexorably. But fast-growing, church-based projects like foodbanks are bringing new hope in communities all round the UK. New initiatives in the churches have potentially huge, positive implications for Britain's future. Ideal for church study groups, this lively, enjoyable, and thought-provoking book looks at 'practical steps … to build a poverty-busting lifestyle'. I thoroughly recommend it."

Rt Hon Stephen Timms MP, Chair, Work and Pensions Select Committee, House of Commons

"Our country has seen a rising tide of poverty, sweeping individuals and families into hardship.… Churches across the land are leading the way in throwing out a lifeline to people in their communities who have been caught up in poverty. Church leaders have great moral authority, not only within the church, but more widely across our country. When they speak out about the injustice of poverty, it sends a powerful message. This book reveals the centrality of tackling the injustice of poverty to the Christian message. It provides a 'how-to guide' for creating 'poverty-busting inclusive church communities'. The book shows how to respond to need with compassion, and demand just changes to the structures that pull people into poverty and keep them there."

Helen Barnard, Acting Director, Joseph Rowntree Foundation

"This is a beautifully timed, needed, and challenging book. I read this during the COVID-19 lockdown, when it was even more poignant as the shelves had emptied and we were all forced to really think about the things we hold dear in our lives.… Chapter 4 asks a question we are currently living out: 'If your church closed its doors today, how long would it take your community to notice?' A chapter worth reading at any time, but particularly pertinent right now.... We all have a God-given responsibility to steward what God has given us—our own resources and his creation—and this is a timely call to act."

Paula Stringer, UK CEO,
Christians Against Poverty

"A Call to Act is a timely follow-up to the brilliant book *The Myth of the Undeserving Poor.* The church's response in this watershed moment as a nation must be informed by grassroots practice. Only then will we have something meaningful to offer on the global stage. I highly commend Martin and Natalie's book to every church leader and church-based community practitioner alike."

Bishop Mike Royal, Co-Chief
Executive, Cinnamon Network UK

"Martin and Natalie have done an excellent job in their latest book, continuing to focus the church very rightly onto the needs of the poor. *A Call to Act* is definitely designed to take us beyond handouts to make us think about providing a genuinely helpful and warm-hearted hand of friendship. More than that, though, it goes beyond interpersonal relationships to challenge us to effect a greater change by engaging with statutory authorities and the environment. We must now take *A Call to Act* seriously as a manual for action, both as individual Christians and as the church."

Revd Dr Hugh Osgood, Moderator,
Free Churches; Co-President,
Churches Together in England

"A book with teeth that will rock you from passivity. I loved the balance of wisdom and exhortation that is flavoured with vulnerability and honest reflection. It challenges at a deeper level and poses questions of Christ followers that must be addressed. Rooted in Scripture and full of helpful application, this book is a fantastic resource for the church at this time. I keep wondering, what would the church look like if we took seriously what is written here? Lord, give us 'a fundamental change of heart concerning the poor'."

Sam Ward, Director of Ministry,
The Message Trust

"In this age of tribalism, when two people from very different backgrounds come together to write something, it's worth taking notice. Here is hard-won wisdom that has been tested in the real world, rather than just preached from a pulpit. At Christians in Politics we see the church (i.e., the people) transforming the culture of politics by choosing to disagree well and put kingdom before tribe, and *A Call to Act* could be a significant step in that direction for you. Quite simply, if you take this book's words seriously, your church and community will be immeasurably better off as a result."

Andy Flannagan, Executive
Director, Christians in Politics

"This is an important, sobering, and challenging book. Martin and Natalie each share their own (very different) backgrounds and life experiences ... and ask difficult questions about the extent to which the modern church is living as it is called to do. This book managed to provoke and challenge me—but not just to feel bad, rather to consider what I might need to do differently, and what that might look like. This book wasn't always comfortable to read, but I'm glad that I did, and I recommend you do too."

Revd Kate Wharton, Assistant National Leader, New Wine England; Author, *Single-Minded*

"Most Christians agree that we are called to love the poor and work for justice, but may not be so clear on what that means in practice. In this short, clear, and often challenging book, Martin and Natalie give a whole range of ways in which we cannot just talk, and think, but act."

Andrew Wilson, Teaching Pastor, King's Church London; Author, *Incomparable*

"Martin and Natalie are experienced practitioners of what they preach. If you are passionate about God's heart towards the poor and disadvantaged, then you will find this book full of wisdom that will help turn your passion into action that truly changes things on the ground."

Phil Moore, Leader, Everyday Church London; Author, Straight to the Heart commentary series

"A vitally important book for our times. In a post-corona world, poverty in our communities is perhaps as big a challenge as it's ever been. This book challenges Christians to put their actions where their faith is. Motivation, encouragement, and ideas that can make a huge difference. This book could change more than just your life, but the lives of the people you meet. An inspirational, transformative, humbling read—but the best bit will happen when you've finished the last page, and then … it's over to you."

Paul Kerensa, British Comedy Award–Winning Co-Writer, BBC's *Miranda, Not Going Out, Top Gear,* ITV's *Royal Variety,* C4's *TFI Friday*

"Serious investors like to invest where they'll get the best returns. They're always on the lookout for good advice. Sometimes they accept the challenge to go against the flow. If you're a Christian looking for kingdom returns, this book will point you on the way. This is a wonderfully, uncompromisingly, practical read. Martin and Natalie mean to make us feel uncomfortable. They leave us with nowhere to run to. How you, personally, choose to respond will reverberate down the generations. It really will. No hype."

Chris Mould, Founder and Chief Executive, Foundation for Social Change and Inclusion; Former Chief Executive, The Trussell Trust Foodbank Network

"I highly recommend Martin and Natalie's latest book to you. I have known them both for a number of years and found, as I was reading their contributions, it was as if they were speaking to me themselves, each in their own voice. This is because what they have written is exactly how they live; what you see is what you get. I strongly advise that, as you read, you take note of what they say. It is spot on, challenging, and makes for deep thinking on changes we need to make, firstly in our thinking, then in the way we put this thinking into practice. Risky living, indeed!"

Angela Kemm, Prophetic Evangelist, Relational Mission & City Church Cambridge

A CALL TO
ACT

A CALL TO
ACT

BUILDING
A POVERTY-BUSTING
LIFESTYLE

MARTIN CHARLESWORTH
& NATALIE WILLIAMS

DAVID C COOK

transforming lives together

A CALL TO ACT
Published by David C Cook
4050 Lee Vance Drive
Colorado Springs, CO 80918 U.S.A.

Integrity Music Limited, a Division of David C Cook
Brighton, East Sussex BN1 2RE, England

The graphic circle C logo is a registered trademark of David C Cook.

The website addresses recommended throughout this book are offered as a
resource to you. These websites are not intended in any way to be or imply an
endorsement on the part of David C Cook, nor do we vouch for their content.

ISBN 978-0-8307-8068-6
eISBN 978-0-8307-8152-2

The Team: Ian Matthews, Jennie Pollock, Jack Campbell, Susan Murdock
Cover Design: Pete Barnsley

Printed in the United Kingdom
First Edition 2020

1 2 3 4 5 6 7 8 9 10

071720

CONTENTS

FOREWORD

Jesus returned to Galilee in the power of the Spirit, and news about him spread through the whole countryside. He was teaching in their synagogues, and everyone praised him.

He went to Nazareth, where he had been brought up, and on the Sabbath day he went into the synagogue, as was his custom. He stood up to read, and the scroll of the prophet Isaiah was handed to him. Unrolling it, he found the place where it is written:

'The Spirit of the Lord is on me,
   because he has anointed me
   to proclaim good news to the poor.
He has sent me to proclaim freedom for the
         prisoners
   and recovery of sight for the blind,
to set the oppressed free,
   to proclaim the year of the Lord's favour.'

Then he rolled up the scroll, gave it back to the attendant and sat down. The eyes of everyone in the synagogue were fastened on him. He began by saying to them, 'Today this scripture is fulfilled in your hearing.' (Luke 4:14–21)

I wonder if this felt like a 'mic-drop' moment? A strong manifesto-setting speech has been delivered from this unlikely, uneducated northern newcomer. It is very clear what his vision and priorities are going to be and who is going to benefit. Today a new leader might make a point of dropping the microphone and folding their arms as a sign that no more needs to be said. Jesus rolls up the scroll of Isaiah and sits down. He has their attention. And for three very good reasons.

First of all, Jesus shows alignment with Scripture. Jesus the Son of God bases his manifesto for the future on what has been revealed in the Bible in the past. Elsewhere he states that he has not come to abolish the law but to fulfil it. Jesus is constantly teaching the Old Testament and explaining his role and his vision using it. Nobody can question it: Scripture is pivotal to his work and his ministry.

Secondly, Jesus recognises his reliance on the Spirit. There is a beautiful mystery in the Bible about how the relationships between God the Holy Trinity work. Jesus here models to us his partnership with the Spirit when it comes to his mission. The work of the Spirit and the pursuit of justice have far too often been separated. Recognising only the first is futile, and only the second can be self-serving. It is the Spirit who authorises and anoints us to meet the needs of those around us.

Thirdly, Jesus prioritises the poor. There is an unmistakable emphasis in Jesus' ministry on helping those in need. Not only is it here in his manifesto, but throughout his ministry the social outcasts are his role models (think of the widow's mite in Luke 21:1–4 and 'blessed are the poor' in Luke 6:20), his most eager followers (think of the lepers, the blind, and the crowds that have nothing to eat), and his preferred company (think of the early disciples and how 1 Corinthians 1:26 says that 'not many [of them] were influential'). This priority is also there in the rest of Scripture where we are reminded again and again to care for the stranger, the orphan, and the widow.

This clear prioritisation led me to found Home for Good, a charity focused on helping children in care to find loving families. It is what drives the work of Jubilee+ and what led Martin and Natalie to write *A Call to Act*. Throughout the book Martin and Natalie emphasise that biblical discipleship and a care for those most in need go together; that loving and serving Jesus means loving and serving those on the margins.

However, it also means more than just caring for those in poverty. It means changing the way we live, the choices we make, and the lifestyle we seek. *A Call to Act* will help churches and individual Christians discover practical ways that they can effect change in their own lives and in their churches, neighbourhoods, cities, and further afield.

It remains vital for the church's mission that we align ourselves clearly with the Scriptures, the Spirit, and the vulnerable. That is why

I love Martin and Natalie's work and why I am excited to commend not just this book but their unrelenting passion to help the church capture God's priorities. They are the real deal—open and honest and committed to finding ways for all of us to take seriously God's compassion for those trapped in poverty.

Dr Krish Kandiah
Founding Director, Home for Good
Author, Speaker, Social Entrepreneur
Lockdown in Oxfordshire 2020

INTRODUCTION

Visit www.calltoact.co.uk for more resources, including videos for your church, small group, or individual study.

On a wintery day in December, Martin and I met in London to go over the draft pages of this book together. As we were chatting, Martin mentioned the first family holiday he remembered: when he was four years old, his family travelled from Pakistan, where they were living at the time, to Sri Lanka. My instant response was, 'Wow, how different our early years were!'

There are many, many ways in which my childhood and background differ from Martin's. He lived in and experienced other parts of the world before hitting his teens. I got my first passport when I turned twenty. He went to public school and an elite university, while I had free school meals courtesy of the State and went to the roughest under-performing secondary school in my community. Whether we look at family stability, education, employment, or many other factors, my childhood and Martin's do not have very much in common.

Martin grew up in relative privilege; I grew up in relative poverty.

However, there is one similarity that has made all the difference: we each encountered Jesus when we were fifteen years old. That turning point for each of us is why—despite our different early experiences of life—we both hold a deep and wholehearted conviction that concern about poverty and injustice is central to the gospel of Jesus Christ. It's something we are firmly committed to, in our work together at the UK Christian charity Jubilee+, and in many other ways in our different local settings.

We believe that a vital element of Christian discipleship is coming to understand that caring for those affected by poverty in our communities is not an optional extra for followers of Jesus. Regardless of our backgrounds, experiences, upbringings—whether we've personally known door-opening privilege or opportunity-limiting poverty—every Christian is called to increasingly reflect God's heart for those who live in poverty or oppression.

But what does this look like, practically?

Martin's experience ...

Sometimes in life you need to take a step back and get everything into perspective. Most of us live at a fast pace. I certainly do. I get up early. I work hard. I have a lot of family responsibilities. I have leisure interests. I have a good many friends. Time passes quickly as a result. Life seems stressed. Life seems focused.

And then sometimes I take a day off and get away from town and go walking in the nearby hills. I live in a rural part of the UK where it is easy to get into the countryside. I turn my smartphone off. Suddenly everything seems to change. All the tough pressures of life seem to fade a little. I reconnect with nature and feel as though I am in a different world; suddenly just being still seems more important than rushing around. I slow down. I reflect. Gone for a while is the pressure of work deadlines, gone is the pressure of advertising, gone is the ring of my phone. Gone is that feeling that I am trying to get somewhere without really knowing where that somewhere actually is!

Then comes the realisation: the things I really enjoy are mostly very simple. Things like a quiet evening in with my wife, playing with the grandchildren, meeting a friend for coffee in town, going for a bike ride, reading a good book, watching a good football match on TV. In many ways, the coronavirus pandemic in the first half of 2020 opened our eyes to how cluttered our lives have become. Due to lockdowns and social distancing, we were no longer able to fill our lives with things that previously felt so essential to us. Through the harsh realities of the pandemic, we learned afresh what really matters in life.

Many of us began to see that we need to rediscover a more straightforward lifestyle. And in order to do so we need to do some hard thinking about the power of consumerism and the materialist culture that threatens to engulf us by telling us that it has the answers to all our needs.

A poverty-busting lifestyle

Poverty usually starts out as a stark economic reality. However, it has a number of other dimensions which frequently go alongside economic need. Many suffer from 'relational poverty'—the lack of stable and healthy family and social networks. This can often be closely connected to a sense of marginalisation and hopelessness which can be described as 'aspirational poverty'. Finally there is 'spiritual poverty'—the lack of a coherent vision for life or set of values to aspire to live by. We have written about these different dimensions of poverty in our previous books[1] and we will be keeping them in mind throughout this book.

Our primary focus in this publication, however, is on developing a poverty-busting lifestyle. Each chapter will focus on a different aspect of the challenge. Chapter 1 was a late addition to this manuscript. Publication was delayed as the COVID-19 strain of the coronavirus spread across the world. Recognising the impact of the pandemic on those in poverty, in particular, Natalie and I submitted the extra chapter several months after the original manuscript. And that is now where we start.

Then in chapter two I offer an overview of current Western culture, particularly in the UK, before looking at some biblical teaching on how Jesus expects his people will live. In chapter three I focus on the need to reconsider our overall approach to living standards and advocate for a radical move towards 'simplicity'. In the next chapter, Natalie considers the key issue of the culture of local churches—arguing for a much greater inclusivity of the socially and/or economically marginalised. In chapter five Natalie goes on to explore the great need and opportunity for churches to engage with decision makers in our local communities on behalf of those in poverty. Then in chapter six I take a close look at consumer purchasing habits and how these can be changed as part of our efforts to address poverty through our day-to-day lives. The final topic, in chapter seven, is the environment. I argue that this is another vital dimension in building a poverty-busting lifestyle because of the social justice implications of the current urgent environmental challenges we face.

Our aim in this book is to think through practical ways in which today's church—by which we mean local churches and individual Christians—can truly reflect the prioritising of those in poverty that Jesus proclaims. We will be considering discipleship—a discipleship which combines active engagement with those in need, advocating for social justice and a willingness to think through and enact the practical implications of living out a poverty-busting lifestyle.

Let's start the journey!

CHAPTER ONE

THE ABRUPT CALL TO ACT OF THE CORONAVIRUS PANDEMIC

The draft text of this book was handed over to the publishers as planned and on time at the end of December 2019. For me (Martin) it is always a great feeling as an author to know that you have finally finished the challenging task of turning your thoughts into the written word. I find the writing process especially challenging since I much prefer to express myself by giving talks than writing books. So on 31 December I remember feeling particularly contented as I settled down at home with my wife to welcome in the New Year.

What I did not know was that on that very day, on the other side of the world, health authorities in Wuhan, the capital of Hubei Province in China, had reported a cluster of strange pneumonia-type cases of unknown cause.[1] Very quickly the scientific community came to understand that a new and dangerous pandemic had broken out, caused by a strain of coronavirus, COVID-19, which had never before been known to infect humans and for which we have no known immunity.

After that, as you will remember, events moved fast across the world as the pandemic spread from country to country at an alarming rate. It turned out that March 2020 was the turning point in the UK—a month that will be forever etched in my memory as one of the most dramatic and challenging in my whole life.

At the beginning of March, political, scientific, and medical leaders in the UK were getting nervous. A few COVID-19 cases were being reported here. The pandemic had reached our shores. The government issued dark warnings about forthcoming impacts on the country. In the second week of March the UK stock market began a dramatic downturn. By the end of the month this had become the biggest single drop in value since the financial crisis triggered by 'Black Monday' in October 1987.[2] This was astonishing and reflected the awareness among investors and economists that the pandemic was going to have dire economic consequences.

Oddly enough, in the middle of March I was due to participate in a local ten kilometre running race. The organisers took public health advice and decided to go ahead on what turned out to be the last day of freedom for social gatherings for many months. Thousands packed into our town centre. It was a good-natured and joyful day.

I met many friends who were fellow runners. My grandchildren cheered me on as I ran past. Everyone was savouring the freedoms that we feared we were about to lose.

The next day the Prime Minister announced the first social distancing restrictions. Panic buying was in full force in our supermarkets, with shortages of toilet paper, hand sanitiser, and many types of food. A week later we were in national lockdown with the economy grinding to a halt, the police monitoring the movement of people, long queues outside supermarkets and buying limits within, and gigantic government bailouts being announced. It was a time of intense fear and uncertainty.

Where was this all going to lead?

My immediate instinct at a time like this is always to be as practical and active as possible. One of my mottos is: 'When in doubt, err on the side of action.' There were lots of issues to think about. As soon as it became clear that COVID-19 was in the UK and becoming a threat, my attention was focused on my family. How could I help protect and support members of my extended family? For example, we quickly took the decision to protect my aged mother-in-law as she entered into medically advised total social isolation at home. As Prime Minister Boris Johnson started to instruct us on social distancing, my attention turned to my neighbours. I quickly visited every home on the street to enquire about how people were doing. There were many long conversations. Various plans were made to support one another in the case of social isolation or illness. As well as my neighbours, there was the local foodbank to consider, for which I have a responsibility as a trustee and church leader. Within days the foodbank team had changed their method of operating dramatically.

An outside reception area for clients was established under the cover of four gazebos. Policies were updated to incorporate social distancing measures. The volunteer team changed in composition as some dropped off due to age, family, or health concerns—while other volunteers came forward quickly. The church leadership team was quick to respond to the new situation and set up all sorts of ways of supporting church members through the forthcoming crisis. And then lockdown came, meaning many more changes to sustain our support for those around us.

This was an intense time as we all adapted to a sudden and dramatic change to our lives. Many readers will remember facing similar issues.

It was in this context that I made one of the strangest phone calls I have ever made. Having spoken with my co-author, Natalie, I called Ian Matthews, our publisher, to make an unusual and bold request. The coronavirus crisis had already led to the delay of the publication of this book by several months, so I asked Ian if we could use the extra time to write another chapter—a chapter addressing some of the significant issues for Christian discipleship that are emerging from the worldwide coronavirus pandemic. I explained that we wanted to focus particularly on lessons related to developing poverty-busting lifestyles. There was a brief pause at the other end of the FaceTime call, and then Ian smiled and said, 'I think we can make that work—and it feels like the right thing to do.' He then went on to tell me that, fortunately, the typesetting had not yet started, so the text could be changed. We, as authors, are so grateful for our publisher's willingness to act quickly and extend the scope of this book at a time of huge national and international upheaval.

The events of early 2020 will fade into history, but the longer-term implications of a world in crisis are now becoming clearer. It is these implications that we want to focus on in this chapter.

Poorest hit hardest

One of the first things I (Natalie) noticed in mid-March was the sense of shock among first-time visitors to my church's foodbank. Many of the people we see throughout the year are familiar with poverty. It's their ongoing reality, something they experience in waves, or something they live in constant fear about, knowing it's never far from their door. But as coronavirus began to impact the UK, a new group started to be referred to the foodbank.

First of all, there was a man beside himself with worry because he had just lost his job in the leisure industry after restaurants, cafés, cinemas, bars, and so on had been instructed to close. Many staff in the leisure industry were laid off with immediate effect. (The British government had not yet announced its Coronavirus Job Retention Scheme.) At the foodbank for the first time, the man told us that he had two pre-school children and had always worked—what would he do now? How would he get another job under the circumstances? He had not experienced need before, and now he was terrified for his family.

A few days later, a very smartly dressed woman queued outside the foodbank. When she reached the front of the queue, she explained quietly that she had enjoyed a very lucrative media career for over twenty years and had never wanted for anything. Overnight her business had collapsed, as one by one every future appointment was cancelled. With a very high mortgage and teenage children at home, she didn't have money that she could get to quickly, and therefore she needed the foodbank. She whispered to me: 'I usually place a couple of tins in the basket at the supermarket when I shop for my family. I have never imagined I would need to come here myself.' The sudden experience of hardship for someone who had never experienced financial difficulties left her looking and sounding utterly shell-shocked.

And then came the announcement that British Prime Minister Boris Johnson was unwell and had tested positively for COVID-19. A week later, he was in hospital. His condition worsened and he was moved to the intensive care unit, before recovering and returning to work a month after he fell sick.

During his spell in hospital, I started to notice a lot of talk in the mainstream media and on social media in particular where people were saying that coronavirus has become 'the great leveller'. The argument was presented that no amount of power, prestige, status, or wealth could protect you from catching COVID-19. Some news programmes in the UK interviewed families coping with the crisis, showing how difficult lockdown was proving for the single mum in a council flat in an inner city and for the married couple trying to home school their children in leafy Sussex while working from home. Distinctions were not made. Instead, the mantra was: 'We're all in this together.'

As Christians, what are we to make of this? While it is obviously true that the COVID-19 strain of the coronavirus is indiscriminate—it has infected and killed thousands regardless of how much money they had, where they lived, or how successful they were—that is not the same thing as it being a great leveller that put us all in the same boat.

While money and power may not be able to protect someone from catching COVID-19 or even from dying from it, they do put the odds of staying healthy in your favour. Globally, nationally, even in our local communities there is not a level playing field when it comes to coronavirus, or life in general. When we think about the international picture, someone who lives in a so-called slum or shanty town is obviously at higher risk of any global pandemic. It is impossible for them to socially distance from those around them, and they are unlikely to have easy access to clean water, much less hand sanitiser. Likewise, for the vast majority of people in the world, healthcare or health insurance is too costly to be within reach. A friend from South Africa explained it starkly to me the other day: 'If you live in what some call "slums" and you get sick with a serious illness, you die.'

Beyond access to free healthcare and being able to socially distance, there has been the impact on employment and personal finances. While a robust, multi-billion-pound package of measures to protect jobs and businesses was rolled out in the UK,[3] there was no government furlough scheme in India, for example, where millions of daily wage earners who went without work for weeks faced hunger.[4] India isn't an exception: across the developing world, vast numbers of people earn a living through market trading, with their income fluctuating day by day under normal circumstances, and no capacity to earn at all under lockdown. In fact, the United Nations World Food Programme predicted in April 2020 that an acute hunger pandemic would follow the COVID-19 pandemic, with an additional 130 million people around the world 'pushed to the brink of starvation by the end of 2020' because of it.[5] Even in wealthier nations, such as the United States, by April 2020 unemployment had already soared to levels not seen since the Great Depression, with 26.5 million people without jobs.[6] But the jobs most at risk across the world are those that pay the least, or offer ad hoc rather than guaranteed shifts.

Even in local communities in the UK, there have been some who were hit harder than others. A disabled single parent living in a high-rise, two-bedroom apartment with two children was likely to find it much harder to self-isolate, social distance, and get essential supplies. Many inner-city parks and green spaces closed during lockdown to deter people from congregating, but the impact on this for families without gardens was significant. Official data from the Office for National Statistics released in May 2020 revealed that the COVID-19 mortality rate among people living in the most deprived areas of the UK was twice that of those living in more affluent parts of the country.[7]

An unforeseen consequence of lockdown has been a spread in violence. Within just a few weeks, reports began to emerge around the world, from the gang rape of a woman in India who had been placed in a school overnight for her safety,[8] to domestic violence soaring globally.[9] In Uganda, for example, five women were murdered by their partners in the first day of lockdown alone.[10] While in the UK, calls to Refuge's National Domestic Abuse helpline had increased by 49 percent and fourteen women and two children had been killed in acts of domestic violence in the first three weeks (more than double the average rate).[11]

The coronavirus pandemic has affected us all, but in very different ways. It is indiscriminate, but it has not been a leveller. We have all faced the same pandemic, but from different starting places, and with varying factors protecting some of us from its impact. While rich and poor, black and white, powerful and powerless, young and old have got sick and even died, privilege has still played a significant part in how the pandemic has played out in our communities and across the world.

Recognising our privilege

From a UK perspective, one of the things that struck me (Natalie) about my own circumstances during lockdown was that I could easily slip into negativity, worry, and even victimhood. In the first six weeks I lost just over a fifth of my income because my consultancy work ceased almost immediately. I live alone, so could easily envy my friends spending lockdown with their families. Not usually a big fan of physical affection, I realised about five weeks into lockdown that I hadn't touched another human being in that time and was actually missing it. Online church was a blessing, but it often brought a stab of sadness too—I found it hard to decide what to do during Communion: should I break bread on my own, or let myself long for the day I could share it with others again? I live in a flat so I don't have a garden; friends nagged me to get outside more. Usually I am fed by other people up to six nights a week—including a forty-six-day run of being cooked for by others in 2019!—so I found it genuinely difficult to adjust to cooking for myself every day. (While tinned macaroni cheese may be ok once a week or fortnight, I'm told emphatically by my friends that it is not a suitable dinner for several times a week.) Five weeks into lockdown I started getting backache from sliding down my sofa as the day progressed while working from home. I noticed after one particularly intense day of seven hours on Zoom that it was making me feel irritable and exhausted to spend so much time talking to people through my laptop screen.

There could have been lots of things to make me feel down and lonely during the coronavirus lockdown, but each of the sentences in the previous paragraph speaks of my relative privilege. I received 75 percent of my income throughout and sometimes even more because my job at my local church increased temporarily as the need for our social action and community engagement projects, which I oversee, went up rather than down. Some of my friends were tearing their hair out by such prolonged and close proximity to their loved ones, especially those who had to balance home schooling several children with working from home. Some people *never* experience physical affection—a rough sleeper once asked me to shake his hand, and when I did, he told me I was the first person to touch him for weeks. I had a strong internet connection that meant I could stream online church, work from home, and catch up with friends—even have online 'parties'. I found vegetables in the freezer (buried under ice cream) and learnt how to have a more balanced diet for myself, without relying on my friends to feed me. More than anything I recognised the privileged position I was in as someone who was able to afford food and at no point had to worry about going hungry. At the same time, it made me incredibly grateful that I am surrounded by people who love to have me over for dinner and genuinely include me in their families.

My gratitude for the things I usually take for granted grew as lockdown went on, and so did my awareness of the needs and hardships of others. I began to realise that this was an opportunity to even more thoroughly put into practice what Martin and I had spent a large part of 2019 writing about (the chapters that follow).

Learning through lockdown

There are many ways in which the coronavirus pandemic and lockdown have had an impact on me when it comes to building a poverty-busting lifestyle. Not just on me, but on churches across the UK, and the world. Jubilee+ (the national charity Martin and I work for) published a booklet in November 2019 called *A Deepening Crisis?*[12] in which we wrote: 'We believe life may get harder for those in poverty in our nation over the coming years … We are working hard to equip churches across the country to prepare for increasing poverty in our communities.' At the time, some questioned the likelihood of what we anticipated, as the economy was relatively strong and politicians were telling us austerity was over. Of course, we didn't see coronavirus coming. But we did have a sense that things were going to get tougher in one way or another for those trapped in poverty.

In the booklet we wrote: 'Now is not a time for us to fear the worst, nor to hope everything turns out ok in the end. Now is the time for us to act.' In many ways that sums up what is was like to live through the peak of the pandemic and the weeks of lockdown. Thousands of churches and tens of thousands of Christians stepped up, and that is just in the UK. Globally, millions of followers of Jesus loved their neighbours more intentionally, shared what they had with those in need, and in some cases put their own lives at risk for the sake of others.

For many of us in the Western world, it started with a reality check about our own money and possessions. When discussing at my church what would happen in terms of staff hours being reduced, voluntary pay cuts, and furlough options, my own knee-jerk reaction was to make the case that I could not afford a pay cut because I had already lost some of my income. It took a few days before I realised this wasn't strictly true. When saying I couldn't afford a pay cut, I had automatically excluded my savings account from my thinking. I had been planning a trip to Atlanta in the US for April, but hadn't booked my flights because I was waiting to see what would happen with coronavirus. The money I would have spent on the trip was sitting in a savings account. But in my thinking—without realising it—I had set that to one side as 'untouchable' for any other purpose. I went back to my church leader to say that I could take a temporary pay cut if necessary after all.

I wonder how many of us automatically do the same: do we have pockets of money that are off limits to God and to those in poverty? When we calculate what we can or cannot afford, are we thinking about the reality of all we have, or have we compartmentalised our finances to the extent that we have convinced ourselves that finances are tight or even that we are hard up? In talking to various people—Christians and those without faith in Jesus—about the impact of coronavirus on their employment and money, it was typically those with the best paid jobs who seemed most worried about losing or needing to sacrifice some of their income. A friend recently pointed out to a group of Christian leaders that sometimes when we are invited to get a takeaway or go out for dinner, we say, 'Sorry, I can't afford it,' when what we mean is not, 'I don't have enough money' but rather, 'I've spent my restaurant budget for this month.' The language we use is important, especially if we want to build a poverty-busting lifestyle that helps people around us who are facing genuine need to be lifted out of hardship. I was reading in Psalm 62 just this morning, before sitting down to write this chapter: 'If riches increase, set not your heart on them' (v. 10 ESV). It is counter-cultural when a rise in our income does not lead to an adjustment of lifestyle and a greater attachment to a lifestyle based on having rather than giving.

Lockdown highlighted to me how much money I spend on things that are not essential. Several friends said the same, as we all commented on how much money we were saving. I found I spent less on cooking for myself than my pre-lockdown expenditure on taking wine to my friends' houses when they fed me! For the relatively affluent, aside from increased food budgets for those who suddenly had their children at home all day every day, most of us found we were saving money because we were not going out with friends, booking day trips or holidays, buying clothes, participating in sports, getting our hair cut, indulging in beauty treatments, visiting coffee shops and pubs, or impulse purchasing while out shopping. These aren't all bad things to spend our money on—some are good. But the point is that not being able to do these things during lockdown gave us scope to recalibrate our thinking. My mum has been encouraging me for years to take a packed lunch to work, and I have always told her I'm too busy. But as soon as our on-site coffee shop closed at my workplace, I suddenly found that on the days I was allowed into the office as a key worker at the foodbank, I did have the time to make lunch before going to work after all. Once lockdown was lifted, of course there were some unavoidable costs that returned immediately, such as petrol once I could travel to work every day and visit friends and family again. But the contrast between my pre-lockdown expenditure and my during-lockdown spending provided an important opportunity to once again soberly assess my habits and take a more faith-filled approach to balancing my needs with the needs of others who have less than I do.

Jesus promised his followers that our essential needs of clothing, food, and drink would be taken care of, but for those who live in the comfortable position of being able to take these for granted, our faith in this is rarely tested. Many Christians whose income was threatened by coronavirus or who for one reason or another did not have an income as we were plunged into the crisis found it revealed the depth of their trust that God would provide all they needed. But for many around us who do not know Jesus, who were suddenly plunged into a depth of poverty and accompanying anxiety that they had not previously known, the pandemic was devastating and, crucially, its impact was not short-lived. Many are now saddled with debt they will struggle to repay, some have not been able to return to their previous employment or rebuild their businesses, others have rent arrears that will live with them for months if they manage to avoid eviction.

However, the impact of coronavirus is not just about money and lifestyle. It is also about loving our neighbours. The pandemic pushed many of us to take this command more literally than we perhaps have for years, if ever. People who previously didn't know their neighbours' names and never spoke with them more than a quick 'hello' and nod of the head made substantial efforts with the people living in their community during lockdown. They gave practical support and made phone calls, set up WhatsApp groups so everyone could check in with each other, offered to pray, and invited those around them to online church. Many of us shared our possessions and we shared our faith. We developed a much healthier and more biblical attitude to community, seeing other people's needs as intrinsically linked to ourselves, rather than separate and optional as a concern.

This wasn't just on an individual level, but was true of local churches too. Most ramped up their community activities. We didn't shrink back under the unique and unprecedented pressures of coronavirus, but we stepped up. Our foodbanks found new ways to source food donations and get it to the most vulnerable in our communities. We worked more closely with local authorities and other statutory agencies, as well as partnered with other voluntary groups. We went the extra mile for those facing hardship, sometimes even putting ourselves at risk because of a sense that the other person's need was greater than our own (imitating the Good Samaritan). And we influenced those with power to make decisions affecting those in need.

In my town, Hastings, what this looked like on the ground was increasing our capacity by doubling our foodbank manager's hours, taking him to full-time, and more than doubling our administrative support so that we could respond to the massive increase in phone calls and emails from those in need, and our partners who were referring them. Our foodbank manager totally reconfigured the physical space in our church building a number of times as the pandemic unfolded. We changed from a collection-only model to a delivery-only service. We started giving out twice as much food per delivery, even though that put a strain on our supplies, which meant we needed to pray more than ever.

What coronavirus meant for another of our projects was that the entire team had to step down temporarily due to being in the 'high risk' category. Baby Basics supports pregnant women who are referred to us by community health visitors and midwives because they cannot afford the essentials they need for when their baby arrives.[13] Many of the pregnant women referred prior to the pandemic were homeless or survivors of domestic abuse or modern slavery. So when the coronavirus crisis happened, these traumatised women whose needs were urgent and desperate at the best of times then had to contend with the additional fear of getting sick or having their baby in a hospital already struggling. Losing all of our regular volunteers overnight meant that others had to step up so this vital service could still run.

Meanwhile our TLG education mentoring project, which involves coaching some incredibly vulnerable seven- and eight-year-olds who were at risk of exclusion from school, also found new ways to work.[14] Dropping off activities and using WhatsApp to support and encourage were vital not only for the children involved but also for their families. Likewise, care packages to the nine survivors of trafficking, and their thirteen children, supported through our Restore initiative meant so much to them during a time when most of the support available had been forced to close due to the need for social distancing.

These are just some examples, but alongside individual church members proactively loving their neighbours, and the church keeping projects open and even increasing the number of people we were able to support, we also worked with others in stronger ways. The church became part of the Hastings Community Hub, a partnership of around seventeen local organisations, which was established rapidly in response to coronavirus. As part of that group, we were invited to chair the Hastings COVID-19 Emergency Food Response Group, which focused its energies on making sure food was getting those facing new or pre-existing poverty, and to put in a bid to DEFRA for £80,000 for food for the most vulnerable in our community, which we were granted.

From Durham in the north to Bristol in the west, from Shrewsbury in the midlands to Lowestoft in the east, I know of scores of stories like ours, where local churches ramped up their work to meet the pressing needs of local people in crisis, as well as building on their existing networks to play their part in supporting those facing poverty—long-term or pandemic-related—in their area. Many, like us, also took a global view, sending financial support to churches overseas so that they could help both their members and those in the community who were suddenly without work, without an income, and without food.

The coronavirus legacy

The peak of the COVID-19 outbreak has passed, but its legacy remains with us. It has damaged people in far-reaching ways. Some have faced bereavement, job loss, or sickness; some have developed mental health conditions, while for others their anxiety, depression, agoraphobia, or OCD has worsened and will not easily or quickly return to their pre-existing levels. Some—including frontline healthcare professionals—are deeply traumatised by what they have seen. A small number have committed suicide.[15] Some have had their lives completely turned upside down by loss of work that has lasted beyond the lockdown period, with no hope of new employment in sight. Some have feared for their lives during lockdown in violent homes. The online distribution of child sexual abuse videos has risen[16]—it's likely that abuse itself has increased too. Marriages have broken down. Debt has racked up. On top of the harrowing impact on people across the country, there's the psychological impact upon us collectively as we have had to face our mortality and lack of control over what happens around us and to us.

But alongside the longer-term impact on people, communities, and nations, there is the potential for a more hopeful and hope-fuelled impact on the church. During the coronavirus pandemic, we were propelled into action, without time to plan or strategise, without really even having time to think and pray. The rest of this book was written before we had even heard of COVID-19, but each chapter seems more relevant in its wake. We are not quite, and maybe never will be, in a post-COVID-19 world, but now that it seems we are beyond the worst of it, this equally isn't a time for the church to shrink back, but to step up. This book was always going to be a call to act for the good of the poorest and most vulnerable in our communities—by building a poverty-busting lifestyle. That call to act is now even more urgent.

Study Topics

1. How did the coronavirus pandemic in the first half of 2020 affect (a) your household, (b) your community, and (c) your nation?

2. What impact does the coronavirus pandemic continue to have on your city or town? What legacy has it left in your immediate location?

3. In what ways did you notice that the pandemic and lockdown were harder for some people than for others? What factors made it a difficult time for you? What factors protected you from the worst of it?

4. How did your church or the churches around you step up to support those in poverty during the pandemic? What were the hardest things for Christians and churches in your area when it came to helping those in need?

5. What can we do now, practically, to reach out to those who continue to live with the consequences of what happened?

6. How did the coronavirus pandemic alter your perspective on the material comforts of your lifestyle that were no longer accessible during lockdown conditions?

CHAPTER TWO

OUR CONTEXT AND OUR CALLING

Looking back in time

Let's start by going back a couple of hundred years. In the UK, where I (Martin) live, things have changed a lot over that time, and that is putting it mildly.

In the 1800s most manual workers laboured over sixty hours per week whether they were men, women, or children. The nineteenth century was filled with legislative efforts to reduce working hours. As a result, the average working day gradually shortened. Today, the current overall average working week is about thirty-eight hours.[1] So we now have a lot more free time than most of our predecessors had—but we mostly don't realise it!

A hundred and fifty years ago most families, apart from a few of the rich, had only a tiny amount of their income available to spend on anything above the necessities of life. Disposable income, as it is called, has shot up over the past century and has enabled most people to spend money on luxuries, hobbies, and holidays to an extent unimaginable to people back then. So we have a lot more money to spend on what we want.

A hundred and fifty years ago the average life expectancy was about forty-one years for men and forty-four years for women.[2] Now it is about seventy-nine years for men and eighty-two years for women.[3] People live much longer. We can plan our futures with more confidence. We have longer retirements. There's more time to focus on things that we think will make us happier. Self-fulfilment is the name of the game.

A hundred years ago there was no universal healthcare system in the UK. Access to healthcare generally depended on having money or paying into an insurance scheme. Now we have a universal healthcare system mostly free at the point of delivery and available to all citizens equally. Healthcare has been transformed. We live healthier lives and have largely eliminated many dangerous killer diseases.

A hundred years ago shopping was hard work. Hardly anyone had cars. Public transport was very limited. Most people went to the local shops on foot to buy the necessities of life. Now we have cars, and a massive range of shops and goods shipped in from all over the world. We do not even have to move out of our homes to shop—we have the internet to help us and home delivery to supply us.

These contrasts are startling. It turns out that our Western societies have, in general, been getting richer and more comfortable. Westerners are now among the most affluent people who have ever lived on this planet.

All this begins to put my life into a more focused perspective. I should be overflowing with thankfulness for the privileges of my life—rather than burdened with stress about the things I would still like to add to it! Yet all around me I see discontented people—people striving to get richer and have more holidays and find that elusive 'self-fulfilment' we keep talking about.

The hard truth is that most Westerners are stressed. Many are under financial pressure. Personal debt levels are soaring. Mental health issues abound. Millions are dependent on anti-depressants. Family relationships are getting weaker. More people than ever are living alone. Social media is creating mass discontent and insecurity. These trends have only been accentuated by the impacts of the recent coronavirus crisis.

Something is wrong. It turns out that wealth alone does not bring real satisfaction and meaning to life. The poet W. H. Auden prophetically coined the phrase 'the age of anxiety' to describe the restless uncertainty of modern Western society.[4]

Looking more closely

Despite the general increase in wealth in our Western societies, there is a big and obvious paradox. Not everyone has been enjoying the benefits. Poverty is stubbornly present if only we have eyes to see it. It is a shocking story and a stark contrast to the burgeoning affluence around us. Yes, there are still a significant number of people who are genuinely poor in countries such as the UK. In particular, there are the long-term unemployed who have become a hidden underclass. Then there are those whose families have broken up. Even when this isn't because of poverty (financial pressure is a leading cause of family breakdown), it can often lead to poverty. Family units are less stable than they used to be. There are those who are effectively excluded because they are unable to use the internet and digital technology. Some have seen their State welfare support reduced in real terms, while others are hugely in debt and cannot work their way out of it.

On top of this, the gap between average Western lifestyles and those in developing countries remains startlingly large. For example, the average annual income per person in the USA is $65,112, compared to $2,172 in India.[5] It is a fact that in many parts of the world there are vast numbers of people in abject poverty—a type of poverty almost never seen in Western countries.[6] Sadly, the worldwide coronavirus pandemic has led to significant further downward pressure on income levels in developing countries.

In the West many churches have been growing in their concern for and support of those in poverty and those who are marginalised. We give to international aid agencies and we have begun to focus more seriously on the poverty on our doorsteps. The rise of the 'foodbank' movement in the UK is a striking example of this.[7] Committed Christians are volunteering in the thousands to help at church-based foodbanks, community cafés, youth-mentoring groups, debt advice services, activities for older people, night shelters, soup kitchens, and much more.

This is a story we have discussed extensively in our two earlier books.[8] It is a positive story. It is an exciting story. However, in this book we are looking behind this to ask deeper, more challenging questions.

Here is a simple observation. While there has been a welcome increase in Christian engagement with those in poverty in recent years, this has not led to much significant reflection on our actual lifestyles.

Has this engagement led us to personally reconsider our own lifestyles and to begin to question our consumerist culture more seriously?

I was visiting a church-based foodbank recently. The car park outside the building was quite small. I found that the way to the entrance was largely blocked by cars—mostly expensive cars. This seemed surprising at first sight. I was later told that these were the cars of the volunteers. So this meant that anyone coming to that foodbank for help would have to run the gauntlet of stylish SUVs and four-by-fours. This is a symbol of a complex relationship between affluence and poverty. These volunteers were sincere, effective, and compassionate. I saw them at work. They were giving up their free time to help needy people. However, their cars symbolised a lifestyle vastly different from those they were seeking to help. Is this significant? Does it matter?

Can we as Christians truly serve those in poverty while still living unchanged consumerist lifestyles? This is a tough question. And it is a question that most of us don't really want to think about.

Looking beyond the media ...

In my childhood in the 1960s, TV was something of a novelty—and it was in black and white! Colour television was viewed as a great wonder when it was first introduced. New channels were added one by one—greeted with great excitement! Those days are long gone. I am absolutely amazed at the number of channels available to me on my TV at home. If we want to, we can have the television on in every room of the house, on large screens and small, throughout the day and night. Watching TV has become a prime leisure activity. This comes with a big price tag—and part of that price tag is the prominence of commercial advertising. Advertising is a major feature of most TV channels. UK public service channels are allowed to show an average of seven minutes of adverts every hour across a day,[9] and this advertising stimulates consumerism.[10]

One vital feature of the modern media world is the rise of the cult of celebrity. Famous, successful, and rich people have an enormous worldwide public audience. They may be millionaires or models, footballers or fanatics, personalities or politicians, actors or action stars—but they are all, in different ways, celebrities. They can attract previously unthinkable numbers of 'followers' through social media. And some are ambitious in self-promotion. The general effect of this phenomenon is to reinforce a cult of success and to promote the idol of materialism.

Our lives are also saturated by the news. Never before in history has so much information been available, easily accessed by so many people so quickly and in so much detail. What is the effect of knowing so much about so many other people and societies? It is helpful to know what is happening in the world—but there are significant problems too. We can easily become de-sensitised to news stories about war, famine, refugees, and outright poverty. It is not easy to take in and reflect on the multiple stories of human hardship. Our inclination is to switch off from them to save us the pain of identification and the guilt of feeling that we should do something. We become paralysed with information overload—leading to inaction.

Then there is the vast new world of social media. As I write, over 2.45 billion people regularly use Facebook[11]—that is about 31 percent of people on the planet.[12] Social media can be a real positive. For example, it is great when seeking to keep in touch with family and friends at a distance. However, the messaging on social media is complex to navigate. Many have found, to their cost, that virtual relationships are a poor substitute for face-to-face relationships. Many people feel more marginalised and undervalued as a result of social media.[13] And it is all very time consuming. It is a serious issue, with studies now showing its impact on mental health, especially among young people, contributing to anxiety, depression, loneliness, aggression, low self-worth, and even suicidal feelings.[14]

It is evident there is a risk that the intense and ongoing world of the media in its many forms can have a huge influence in the way we think and act as Christians. Often we do not realise the extent to which we are being shaped by the media. One of the key ways the media shapes us is to make us passive. We watch the world go by from our armchairs. Meanwhile we begin to think purely in terms of consumption. Should we be considering what media we want to use and for what purpose?

In the same way that people tend to have a newspaper or TV channel of choice when it comes to news, so we tend to stick to our preferences online. In our earlier book *The Myth of the Undeserving Poor*, we explored in detail how the media influences our thinking around a number of issues relating to poverty. We concluded, sadly, that there is 'a sobering challenge in terms of why we believe what we believe … The influence of our news sources is a particular concern.'[15]

Christians cannot afford to let other people do our thinking for us. We are called upon to take a different approach, to be radical:

> Therefore, I urge you, brothers and sisters, in view
> of God's mercy, to offer your bodies as a living sac-
> rifice, holy and pleasing to God—this is your true

and proper worship. Do not conform to the pattern of this world, but be transformed by the renewing of your mind. Then you will be able to test and approve what God's will is—his good, pleasing and perfect will. (Rom. 12:1–2)

How do we 'renew our minds' and get free from the 'pattern of this world'? First and foremost by taking another, closer, look at the life and teaching of Jesus.

Looking to Jesus ...

The Gospels are filled with surprise encounters people had with Jesus. Here's one. Simon Peter was a fisherman. When he had first met Jesus, he had begun the journey of faith (John 1:40–42). Then one day, when Peter had come to the end of an unsuccessful night shift fishing on the Lake of Galilee, he was washing his nets and preparing for a quick sleep when Jesus happened to pass by. Jesus surprisingly asked Peter to get back into his boat and have another go at getting a decent catch. Peter and his fishing partners did this and found they had caught so many fish that the nets began to break! This is a well-known story. However, it is the outcome which is really interesting. As Peter was thinking about this extraordinary event, Jesus invited him to give up his livelihood, get on the road with him, and travel around as part of Jesus' inner circle of followers. Here's what happened: 'So [Peter, James and John] pulled their boats up on shore, left everything and followed him' (Luke 5:11). That is a truly amazing event. What could possibly persuade Peter and his fishing partners to give up their security and income?

This was discipleship—the call to follow and obey Jesus. Discipleship is about lifestyle.

Christian discipleship is about following Jesus and letting him be our Lord in life. This is what Jesus invites us to do when he says: 'Take my yoke upon you and learn from me' (Matt. 11:29). It is a conscious decision to become an active, committed follower rather than just a casual church attender or a private believer. Many Christians have never thought of themselves as disciples in this specific sense. Arguably, the majority of church attenders in the Western world may not be true disciples of Jesus after all. They attend churches either hoping that some personal needs will be met, or out of cultural tradition or for some specific social benefit. In any culture, there's a danger we can go along to meetings out of obligation, tradition, or duty, or the desire to have our own needs met, rather than because we are genuine disciples who have submitted our lives to the lordship of Christ.

Jesus calls us to a radical commitment.

Disciples follow the example of their leader. They try to live lives which reflect the values and teaching of their leader. To understand what this means, we need to immerse ourselves in the New Testament—but particularly in the four Gospels. Even a casual reading will tell us that following Jesus as a disciple involves deep commitment:

> Then Jesus said to his disciples, 'Whoever wants to be my disciple must deny themselves and take up their cross and follow me. For whoever wants to save their life will lose it, but whoever loses their

life for me will find it. What good will it be for someone to gain the whole world, yet forfeit their soul? Or what can anyone give in exchange for their soul? For the Son of Man is going to come in his Father's glory with his angels, and then he will reward each person according to what they have done.' (Matt. 16:24–27)

Here we have some of the key themes of discipleship. Firstly, there is self-denial ('deny themselves'). Personal self-fulfilment in the modern sense is not on the agenda for disciples. Secondly, there is the willingness to face opposition ('take up their cross') as a result of public identification as a disciple of Jesus. No private, personal faith here. Faith is lived out in public as we witness for Christ. Thirdly, there is a decision to reject the materialist dream of acquiring extensive wealth ('to gain the whole world'). This discipleship lifestyle is only possible if we get the right perspective on our lives. Our present life is not the only one. Eternal life with Christ awaits us after we die. This certainty provides security and also the hope of a 'reward' for our faithfulness in this life—however hard that life may have been.

To get an understanding of what this might mean, we need to start by noticing what Jesus said at the beginning of his ministry. This sets the agenda for all that follows. His first recorded words of preaching are: 'The time has come … The kingdom of God has come near. Repent and believe the good news!' (Mark 1:15). Jesus announced that God's 'kingdom' was arriving among mankind and that this would demand radical changes—changes of attitude, belief, and action.

But what exactly would this 'kingdom' bring to mankind? Jesus provided a direct and powerful answer to this question shortly after his opening proclamation. He returned for the first time to his hometown, Nazareth, after he had been baptised by John the Baptist, empowered by the Holy Spirit, and launched into his ministry by the words of the Father.[16] His family, friends, and neighbours were extremely interested to know what was happening to Jesus. As he went into the local synagogue to worship on the Sabbath day as he had done for many years, they all pressed into the building to hear what he might say. Luke records the incident vividly for us:

> He went to Nazareth, where he had been brought up, and on the Sabbath day he went into the synagogue, as was his custom. He stood up to read, and the scroll of the prophet Isaiah was handed to him. Unrolling it, he found the place where it is written:
>
> 'The Spirit of the Lord is on me,
>   because he has anointed me
>   to proclaim good news to the poor.
> He has sent me to proclaim freedom for the
>   prisoners
>   and recovery of sight for the blind,
> to set the oppressed free,
>   to proclaim the year of the Lord's favour.'
>
> Then he rolled up the scroll, gave it back to the attendant and sat down. The eyes of everyone in

the synagogue were fastened on him. He began by
saying to them, 'Today this scripture is fulfilled in
your hearing.' (Luke 4:16–21)

So it turns out that this 'kingdom' is going to have a radical
impact on those in poverty, the sick, and the marginalised. They will
be the primary recipients of God's grace through his coming kingdom. When we read through the gospel accounts, we see many ways
in which Jesus brought this into reality: physical healing, the forgiveness of sins, provision of material needs, giving hope and meaning in
life, freedom from oppressive evil forces …

It is not our task here to follow this amazing story in any detail.
Our previous books looked more closely at the practicalities of
how this worked out in Jesus' life and in the early church.[17] What
we need to note are some of the more obvious implications for
Christian discipleship. Two things are coming into focus already.
Firstly, discipleship involves self-denial and a decision to let go
of the pursuit of materialistic comfort and wealth. Secondly, discipleship involves enabling many poor and marginalised people to
receive the kingdom of God and embrace the power of the saving
death and resurrection of Jesus. This involves not just crisis support
but a focus on changing societal structures when they cause oppression of those in poverty.

With this in mind let's now turn to a key text for discipleship—
the so-called Sermon on the Mount, found in Matthew 5–7.
Matthew's gospel is constructed as a discipleship manual for the
early church. Matthew makes a deliberate attempt to highlight Jesus'
teaching on discipleship.[18] The Sermon on the Mount is vital in our

attempt to understand what it means to be a disciple of Jesus. We are going to focus on Matthew 6, which addresses the lifestyle issues we are seeking to understand.

In the first half of the chapter, Jesus describes how his disciples should carry out three regular religious practices—giving to those in need, private prayer, and fasting from food (Matt. 6:1–19). It is interesting to note how these three practices are considered normal and commonplace by Jesus. Yet how many Christians discipline themselves to pray regularly in private? How many of us fast regularly? And how many of us give to those in poverty regularly? The focus in this passage is on doing these things as discreetly as possible—so no one notices, if possible. The motive is to please God the Father and to receive a reward from him.

So it appears from this teaching that disciples will regularly give to those in poverty. How will this be done? This is for us to work out in our contexts. It is the regularity and the motive that matters. Through our lifestyle of giving, the kingdom of God will come to those in need.

This sounds fine in principle—but very hard to live out in practice. Jesus knew this and his next teaching addresses the root issue. In Matthew 6:19–24, he identifies one of the primary issues of discipleship. It turns out that 'treasure'—which could be money, property, or other possessions—functions like a huge psychological and spiritual power in our lives. It exploits our fears for the future in particular and offers the safety of a life full of materialistic treasures. Disciples are those who have turned their backs on the attractions of 'treasure' and are putting their trust in God as their Father as they take risks with their material security.

Jesus concludes this revolutionary teaching by focusing on our tendency to be anxious about our material provision (Matt. 6:25–34). 'Therefore I tell you, do not worry about your life' (Matt. 6:25). He offers a radical alternative to the persistent anxiety about money that besets us all: 'But seek first his kingdom and his righteousness, and all these things will be given to you as well' (Matt. 6:33). We can't just decide not to worry about money and about making ends meet. It doesn't work like that! There is a more radical alternative. This is to focus our energies on advancing God's 'kingdom' and his 'righteousness' which will naturally raise people out of poverty. How surprising to find that the antidote to worry about our money and possessions is actually to invest our lives into the kingdom that is good news for those facing poverty. God is always active in his mission to reach people and bring them to salvation. We are called, as disciples, to be partners and co-workers with him. As we work out what this means for us and orientate our lives to obey that calling, we are promised that God will meet our material needs.

Looking to the early church ...

So how did this process work out in the early church? We get a really good insight from the apostle Paul as he writes to his associate Timothy and advises him how to handle issues in the churches he is looking after.

First, Paul talks about getting the right attitude to money and wealth:

> But godliness with contentment is great gain. For
> we brought nothing into the world, and we can

take nothing out of it. But if we have food and clothing, we will be content with that. Those who want to get rich fall into temptation and a trap and into many foolish and harmful desires that plunge people into ruin and destruction. For the love of money is a root of all kinds of evil. Some people, eager for money, have wandered from the faith and pierced themselves with many griefs.

But you, man of God, flee from all this, and pursue righteousness, godliness, faith, love, endurance and gentleness. Fight the good fight of the faith. Take hold of the eternal life to which you were called when you made your good confession in the presence of many witnesses. (1 Tim. 6:6–12)

The best way to live as a Christian, Paul says, is to cultivate an attitude of contentment with your lifestyle. Thankfulness for our basic physical needs being met is a great way to develop an attitude of 'contentment'. However, if we are basically content with our standard of living, there will always be the temptation of 'the love of money'. So what do we do if we find ourselves thinking obsessively about earning more, going up in the world, keeping up with richer friends or neighbours? Paul is clear—turn away decisively even from this thought pattern. Instead, actively pursue God's kingdom— 'righteousness, godliness, faith, love, endurance and gentleness.' Fighting for the advancement of God's kingdom is good news for those in poverty, says Paul, then you won't be tempted to think so much about enhancing your own lifestyle and personal comfort.

It is a radical message. But it echoes closely Jesus' teaching. This is discipleship.

Interestingly, Paul then goes on to tell Timothy how to teach and guide richer people in the church:

> Command those who are rich in this present world not to be arrogant nor to put their hope in wealth, which is so uncertain, but to put their hope in God, who richly provides us with everything for our enjoyment. Command them to do good, to be rich in good deeds, and to be generous and willing to share. In this way they will lay up treasure for themselves as a firm foundation for the coming age, so that they may take hold of the life that is truly life. (1 Tim. 6:17–19)

Here is some direct guidance for those Christians who seek to follow Christ but have a good standard of living and more money than they need to live on. Paul starts by warning them not to trust their wealth to meet all their needs or to make them feel self-important. Rich people, rather, should build up their active faith in God—in other words, they should make their spiritual lives really strong. Then, having done that, they need to do two practical things. Firstly, adopt a lifestyle that focuses on helping people in need in any way they can. Secondly, they need to specifically give some of their money away to help to those who are in poverty.

What might that look like in practice for us today?

Study Topics

1. Have you ever thought of yourself as a disciple? How might it change your daily life if you did?

2. What areas of your life has God been talking to you about as you read this chapter? What provoked an emotional response in you? Are there any areas where he might be prompting you to live more simply?

3. What holds you back from a lifestyle of generosity? How does Matthew 6 speak to your concerns?

4. How often do you thank God for your material possessions and for the richness he has given you in other areas of your life (health, family, friends, education, etc.)?

CHAPTER THREE

A LIFE OF SIMPLICITY

Two things I ask of you, LORD;

    do not refuse me before I die:

keep falsehood and lies far from me;

    give me neither poverty nor riches,

    but give me only my daily bread.

Otherwise, I may have too much and disown you

    and say, 'Who is the LORD?'

Or I may become poor and steal,

    and so dishonour the name of my God.

        (Prov. 30:7–9)

Where do we go from here?

Now comes the hard work—and the excitement of the journey! If we want to be disciples of Jesus living in affluent countries in the twenty-first century, we are going to have to find a way of connecting the teaching of Jesus and Paul on lifestyle issues with the complexities and terrible inequalities of our modern world. We should not be motivated by guilt in setting about this task. Rather, we should be driven by a passionate desire to follow Jesus wholeheartedly as disciples, compelled by a joyful willingness to make sacrifices for people much poorer than we are.

Let me tell you something of my story. I (Martin) grew up in a secure middle-class home in England. My family always had enough money to live on. We always had money to spend on holidays. We lived in a comfortable home. When I became a Christian at the age of fifteen, I quickly became thoroughly committed to Christian discipleship. I read the Bible eagerly. I joined a strong church. I told my friends about my faith. I was taught that giving to my church was a good idea based on the Old Testament concept of 'tithing'—so I started giving 10 percent of my income to the church.

There was only one problem. No one had told me much about how to respond to materialism or about the poorer parts of our society or about how to engage with the terrible suffering created by poverty worldwide. I had a lot to learn. It is very easy to tick the boxes of outward Christian living without having a fundamental change of heart concerning poverty.

Then, aged eighteen, I went on a gap year project to South Africa—and everything changed. I encountered the harsh reality of economic and racial injustice in no uncertain terms through the apartheid regime in power at the time. My whole perspective on discipleship was shaken up and challenged. I re-read the New Testament and discovered to my surprise all of Jesus' teaching about the cost of discipleship and the need to take a radical approach to money and materialism. I had simply not noticed it before! Then, while at university, I heard a visiting American preacher in my church. His name was Ron Sider, the author of an influential book at the time—*Rich Christians in an Age of Hunger*. That was a game-changer for me as it radically exposed the way Christians in the West can live affluent lives without engaging with the vast needs of the developing world around them.

This all took place more than forty years ago. Since then I have been on a challenging life journey from student to school teacher, to shop manager, to church pastor, to social activist, to leadership trainer and charity leader. Early on I married Jane, and we have raised three children, who are now adults. In every phase of my life, I have had to try to work out what it means for me and my family to follow the radical path of discipleship laid out by Jesus. My wife and I have tried to live out this journey together. Her experience of a childhood spent living in various remote places in East Africa has always given her a strong sense of proportion when it comes to money.

There has been a lot to learn about 'simplicity' over the years. What follows represents the six most important lessons which have shaped me—six aspects of the journey. I hope you find them helpful as you walk down a similar path of discipleship.

From complexity to simplicity

Most of us like buying and collecting things. What is it for you? Food? Clothes? Household gadgets? Something for the car or toys for the kids? For me the biggest buying interest is books! I love to read and to refer to books. They become like friends, and they each get a little home on one of my many bookshelves. However, I had a shocking experience recently. I am trying to reduce the number of books I own due to lack of space. I was going through my collection and I discovered, to my horror, that there were quite a few that I have not referred to in over ten years—and some have not been opened in twenty years! So why do I keep them? It is a good question. We all develop unseen emotional attachments to things we own. Sometimes those unspoken emotional ties need breaking. This all came to a crunch a few weeks ago when I went through all my bookshelves and decided which ones had to go. It took such a long time to decide. Each book represented memories or some form of emotional attachment! It was a struggle to let them go, but now they can be of use to someone else rather than gathering dust on my shelves. Getting rid of them didn't directly lift anyone out of poverty, but it helped to detach my heart from regarding my possessions as treasures and freed it up to treasure the things of the kingdom instead.

Life is made complex by having so much choice. The more choice there is, the more we tend to buy. The more choice there is, the more likely we are to buy things we do not really need. Advertising creates a sense of dissatisfaction with what we own and urges us on to buy more and more things.

Let's take the question of clothing. Fashion is heavily driven by the media and has led to huge pressures, especially on women and young people, to change or update their wardrobes almost continually. This is complex. It is costly. It leads to huge wastage as good-quality garments are often consigned to the bin or sent for recycling when they have hardly been worn by their owners. Shockingly, even the ill-fitting new clothes we return to retailers often also end up unused or even in landfill.[1] Fashion trends like this extend far beyond clothing—to food, to cars, to smartphones, to music, to leisure activities ... and much more.

The contrast between complexity and simplicity became apparent to many of us in the Western world during the coronavirus pandemic, when we spent less on luxuries and possibly spent more on essentials. The difference between what is needed and what is superfluous was writ large on supermarket shelves that were empty of toilet paper but remained full of Easter eggs.

However, under normal circumstances, we are involved in a complex materialistic society with multiple ways of spending money. We get drawn in. Often we do not think clearly about decisions we are making. For those with any disposable income, buying is so easy. It is usually only a click away. If we have the money (or credit), we can sit in the comfort of our armchairs at home and buy almost anything we think we want. So little effort. Such big consequences.

It is time for a rethink. It is time for a discipleship perspective. It is time to move from complexity to simplicity. But what do I mean by simplicity? Here is my working definition: *simplicity of lifestyle means basing your standard of living primarily on what you genuinely need to live viably in your society.* Our necessary costs of living vary a lot according to where we live and how much housing, food, and other basic needs cost us. It is good to calculate this as accurately as possible. However, the implication of this is to realise that many things we spend money on are not strictly necessary to viable living—they are extras. This way of thinking involves asking questions of purchasing habits that involve luxuries and things that make no practical difference to our lives. However, 'simplicity', as I have described it, is closely linked to the discipleship way of life which Jesus outlines in

Matthew chapter 6. Simplicity involves focusing on genuine material needs and seeing material things as being in the service of the kingdom of God rather than as an end in themselves.[2] Simplicity involves a decision not to collect or hoard material wealth just for the sake of providing personal security, comfort, or status.[3]

Here's a good way to start on the journey towards simplicity. Go through your personal or family budget and all your regular financial outgoings. There are many websites and apps which can help.[4] Ask yourself if you really need everything you are spending money on. This could be a demanding or tense process—but it is really worth doing regularly. I keep a regularly updated family budget, and this enables my wife and me to quickly evaluate how much money we spend on essentials, luxuries, giving, and miscellaneous extras. I have to do some painful thinking every time I go through this budget! Luxuries have a tendency to increase, and giving does not usually follow suit unless clear decisions are made. Almost everyone is surprised by some of the amounts of money they spend and what they've spent it on when they analyse their budgets in this way.

Once you have looked at your finances, how about going through your possessions at home? This can be a sobering thing to do as well. Various members of the family or household will value things differently. I guarantee that any family or group of friends going through this exercise will come to a point when they say to each other: 'Where did this come from?' or 'Why on earth did you buy this?' or 'I had completely forgotten I even owned this!' You will be amazed at the results.

A good way to move towards the goal of simplicity is to base your household budget expenditure primarily on what you think you need to live viably. Then, as time passes, if you get into the position that your income is going up (higher earnings) or your expenditure is going down (mortgage paid off, receiving an inheritance, children leaving home, etc.), you know that you do not necessarily need to increase your expenditure. In this way you are choosing the path of simplicity. Then you will have more income available to share and to give away to those in need.

A few days ago a friend asked me for advice on house-buying as his family planned to move due to work. Should they buy a large house with a large mortgage? Should they move into a desirable area? How near should they live to the children's schools? These are common questions, and it is interesting to think of them through the lens of a biblical 'simplicity' mind-set. My friend had some equity in his last house and was able to consider a range of housing options. This is not the case for a lot of people. Many younger people are struggling to even get on the housing ladder due to the very high cost of housing. Property ownership is not an intrinsic good. However, for those who have the financial resources to choose between a variety of housing options, it is worth thinking carefully about what we actually need and what is just for pure comfort. The 'simplicity' mind-set causes us to ask different questions about such decisions. Most of us think of our homes as our safe havens, but what if we started to think of them as a refuge for others?

From self-protection to generosity

Money offers to protect us from risk and danger. That is part of its attraction. It sounds like a good deal, doesn't it? We all want to be safe and secure in life. Private health insurance will get us help when we have a medical emergency, income insurance will give us a regular income if we suddenly lose our jobs, accident insurance will pay for the things we break, a good pension will bring us the money we need in retirement …

Some insurance policies can be really helpful—and some are legally required. However, the question we have to ask is about how far we go down this way of thinking? How much of your life do you need to insure? How much of your income should go into self-protection? When are we called to take *significant risks and trust God financially?*

There is obviously no simple answer to this question. However, it is a real question if you are someone who lives with a reasonable income in an affluent nation. What is more, commercial advertising exploits our fears and continually seeks to persuade us that we need to be safer and that we need to protect ourselves against all eventualities.

Let's compare all this to the teaching of Jesus. He calls on his disciples not to give in to anxiety—or self-protection: 'Therefore I tell you, do not worry about your life, what you will eat; or about your body, what you will wear. For life is more than food, and the body more than clothes' (Luke 12:22–23). Then he goes on to describe what happens when anxiety is replaced by faith: 'Do not be afraid, little flock, for your Father has been pleased to give you the kingdom. Sell your possessions and give to the poor. Provide purses for yourselves that will not wear out, a treasure in heaven that will never fail, where no thief comes near and no moth destroys. For where your treasure is, there your heart will be also' (Luke 12:32–34).

Disciples of Jesus face a challenge. How much should we follow the cultural tendency to use money as a way of protecting us from danger? And how much should we live by faith, trusting God for our protection and well-being, thus releasing significant amounts of money to share with others and give to those in poverty? Every person and every family has to work this issue out for themselves. There are no simple answers. However, our starting place needs to be a robust faith in God's provision and protection rather than a slavish adherence to cultural pressure to protect ourselves from as many risks as possible.

My wife and I have thought long and hard about this and decided, for example, that while it is very wise and practical to pay into a pension scheme, we will try to avoid an attitude of self-protection, which would cause us to tie up a significant amount of money in insurances and over-cautious savings. Over the years we have made calculated decisions to give money away which we could have saved. We have also cancelled some insurance policies and resisted many tempting offers to insure specific household appliances and possessions.

From comfort to proximity

What you don't see, you don't think about.

The people you really think about are usually the people you relate to. And the people you relate to are generally like you—similar interests, similar employments, similar social background, similar racial background, similar economic background ...

Have a think about it for a moment. Who are your best friends? Who are the ten people you know best? Are they similar in outlook to you? I am sure most of them will share many similarities. That is what tends to bring us together as people.

Most societies have physical divisions that separate people. The biggest such division is housing. Where you live is usually a defining cultural marker in your society. This was starkly evident during the coronavirus pandemic. Poorer people generally live in poorer housing districts that are known for their poverty, are cheap to live in, and are firmly avoided by anyone who has enough money to choose to live in more comfortable districts. We all know this happens. In some parts of the developing world, the difference between poor housing and better housing is enormous. In the Western world these divisions are less extreme, but they are still there. I have the same feeling of crossing from one culture to another when I walk into a poor inner-city estate in a British city as I did a few years ago when I walked into Kibera, which is one of the largest slums in Africa and situated in Nairobi, Kenya.

The issue here is 'proximity'. Most people prefer the comfort of being with people similar to themselves and with similar income levels, rather than with people who are culturally different—and particularly, much poorer. We are told that upward mobility is always good—but is it? Natalie will explore this further in the next chapter.

We have a proximity problem. It is hard to understand people you do not know. Those of us in the UK live in a society where many of us don't even know the names of any of our neighbours, let alone people who might be slightly removed from us by neighbourhood or social status.[5]

Jesus' life is a fascinating study in proximity. As he travelled around ancient Israel, he continually crossed boundaries and breached social divides. He lived among ordinary people and reached out to the social outcasts. He gladly socialised with the ostracised tax collectors, he was happy to meet prostitutes, he welcomed little children, he reached out to racially segregated Samaritans. Lepers were another notable example. Leprosy was a much-feared disease in those days—and for good reason. It was easy to catch from bodily contact, and there was no cure available. Lepers suffered from terrible sores, numbness, loss of mobility, blindness, and the rejection of society in general. They were forced to live in their own little communities outside towns and villages. Yet Jesus seemed quite happy to sit in close proximity with lepers, to touch them, to have them near him.

> While Jesus was in one of the towns, a man came along who was covered with leprosy. When he saw Jesus, he fell with his face to the ground and begged him, 'Lord, if you are willing, you can make me clean.'
>
> Jesus reached out his hand and touched the man. 'I am willing,' he said. 'Be clean!' And immediately the leprosy left him. (Luke 5:12–13)

The path of discipleship is the path of proximity. Christians should be always open to building relationships and friendships across the divides created by our society. This is not about just helping people—it is about knowing them and treating them with friendship and dignity.

About ten years ago a man called Tom walked into our church. He had serious problems. He was heavily in debt. His marriage had failed. He lived alone and was prone to depression. Although he had a job, his life was in a mess. He came from a poor social background and had spent much of his leisure in his earlier life in pubs, where he had become something of a fighter. To cut a long story short, he came to a living faith, joined the church, and has become a firm friend. We often laugh over the fact that our social backgrounds are totally different. This friendship has deeply enriched my life. Tom helps me to understand life from the point of view of the disadvantaged, the underdog, and those in need.

Proximity through friendships and relationships with many different people has been an important part of my journey.

All this has lifestyle implications. It may affect where we live. We may feel called to go to live in the poorer parts of our town, city, or district. It may affect who we spend time with. It may affect how we make friendships. It could even affect who lives in our homes—whether that means fostering, adoption, or taking in survivors of slavery or refugees. Intentionally increasing our proximity will call us to step out of our comfort zones.

From individualism to community

Church attendance is generally falling in the West. This decline has been going on for a long time. Currently, regular church attenders in the UK are estimated at only about 11 percent of the adult population.[6] This decline is a well-known story—leading some to write off the church altogether.

However, here is the surprise. Whenever people are surveyed concerning their religious beliefs, there turns out to be a surprisingly high number of 'believers' out there. But most of them are not part of actual church communities. They are at home on Sundays ... or maybe shopping ... or perhaps at the gym or with friends. Their faith, at whatever level it exists, is individual and private. It's what they believe in their own minds; it is the ethical standards they operate under at work; it is the background to their family life. But most of them are not to be seen in churches on Sundays.

The reasons for this are not too hard to find. The West has become more and more individualistic in many ways. Families are less robust, more people than ever live alone, and social media is creating a whole new world of 'virtual' relationships which can be conducted without leaving your armchair or opening your door to anyone else. (In fact, in the early days of coronavirus lockdown in the UK, it was estimated that one in four went to 'online' church—a big increase when church could be enjoyed from the comfort of your own home.)[7]

This trend towards privatised faith needs to be reconsidered—it is not compatible with biblical discipleship.

So why can't you be a follower of Jesus without having to go through the inconvenience of commitment to a local church? The answer is simple. Jesus built a discipleship community during his three years of public ministry. It was based around the twelve disciples, but there were many others attached to Jesus' discipleship community. They spent a lot of time together. They travelled together. They worked together. They helped each other. This was the prototype of the dynamic church community which was to come into being on the day of Pentecost.[8] It is noticeable that just before Jesus died he taught his disciples to be radically committed to one another:

> As the Father has loved me, so have I loved you. Now remain in my love. If you keep my commands, you will remain in my love, just as I have kept my Father's commands and remain in his love.

I have told you this so that my joy may be in you
and that your joy may be complete. My command
is this: love each other as I have loved you. Greater
love has no one than this: to lay down one's life for
one's friends. (John 15:9–13)

And there is another huge problem with modern privatised faith. This current trend stands in the way of meaningful care for those in poverty. The wonderful thing about a healthy church community is that it mobilises individuals to work together in teams, enabling us to achieve more significant outcomes than individuals alone could achieve. This may seem very obvious to state—but it needs reiteration in the light of the widespread abandonment of commitment to local churches in the West.

Let me take my church as an example. We are privileged to have a strong membership including people of all ages and from a variety of social and ethnic backgrounds. This then enables us to run various social projects, including a foodbank, a parent and toddler group, a bereavement service, a senior citizens' group, various life skills groups—and more. Each project is served by a diverse team which deploys all sorts of gifts. Almost all our helpers are volunteers. Such teamwork would be extremely hard to achieve if our church did not exist and if all our current members were simply individual Christians living out their faith privately.

The community of faith is primarily the local church. However, alongside thriving local churches, we must remember the local Christian charities which enable Christians from various churches (and others) to work together for some common social project across an area. Also, there are national charities and organisations which extend this principle across the whole country.

However, the bottom line is clear. Individualised faith won't work in terms of a radical and effective care for those in poverty. Disciples work out their faith in the communities of local churches—and this is where the most effective outreach to the marginalised almost always takes place. Everything is better done in community.[9]

From spontaneity to strategy

Many Christians have little sense of focus in their approach to those in poverty. We are generally concerned about poverty and need. We often feel slightly guilty for not doing enough to help. We may be willing to give some money if asked. We may well respond to a disaster relief initiative we see in the media, and many of us gave generously to various coronavirus-related appeals at the height of the pandemic. We probably support a charity or two in a modest way. However, for most of us, the overall amount we give to supporting those in poverty is generally very small compared to our other outgoings.

It takes strategy to truly help those living in poverty.

Let's think about the 'Good Samaritan' in Jesus' parable. The love and generosity he showed to a complete stranger from another racial background is remarkable. This fact is what we tend to focus on when we discuss this amazing parable. However, there is another aspect of the story that is usually overlooked. Let's go back and have another look at the actions of the Samaritan:

But a Samaritan, as he travelled, came where the man was; and when he saw him, he took pity on him. He went to him and bandaged his wounds, pouring on oil and wine. Then he put the man on his own donkey, brought him to an inn and took care of him. The next day he took out two denarii and gave them to the innkeeper. 'Look after him,' he said, 'and when I return, I will reimburse you for any extra expense you may have'. (Luke 10:33–35)

When the Samaritan man was faced with the urgent need of the stricken man, he first of all showed spontaneous compassion and did what he could to help him at the side of the road. This in itself was a lot more than the other travellers on the road had done! Sometimes we read this story as if this was the central event, but fail to notice that the Samaritan immediately did something much more radical and costly—he made a plan. He decided to take the man with him and stop over at the nearest travel hostel and spend some time helping the man in the next stages of recovery. Having done that, he left the man in the care of the innkeeper until he could return some time later. This was a strategic plan! It involved a significant amount of money. The first payment to the innkeeper (two denarii) represented about two days of an average working man's wage. It wasn't small change. And he was willing to pay more to the innkeeper when he returned. Then there was the time spent helping the man and the resulting interruption of his travel plans. It also involved working in active partnership with the innkeeper which, no doubt, had to be planned and discussed carefully.

Really helping people generally requires strategy—and a longer-term commitment. In an age which favours quick fixes and instant results, it is easy to think that poverty can be resolved quickly. It can't. Westerners have tended to hope that giving large amounts of money can solve serious issues of poverty in the developing world. Experience has shown us that this is generally not the case. It needs a more comprehensive strategy.

Discipleship implies a lifestyle of long-term commitment to the things God calls us to do.

Here is an example from my own experience. During a meeting in a leadership conference in 1995, I suddenly experienced a remarkable spiritual 'vision'. Such things don't normally happen to me! It was very surprising. In my mind I saw a picture of myself sitting around a dining room table for Christmas dinner with my family seated with me. The table was laden with rich food. Then suddenly, in the far distance, I saw a handful of poor women. Their dress and manner suggested that they were Eastern Europeans or Russians. They called out to me urgently: 'Share your bread with us!' I found myself moved to tears after this experience and wondered what it might mean. Shortly afterward my church had the unexpected opportunity to be involved in some mission work in Ukraine. I visited the area and saw women just like those I had seen in the spiritual vision. I knew that we were called to work in this country. That was over twenty years ago: our church set up a charity providing humanitarian support through local churches to needy groups there throughout the past two decades. This strategy was born out of a combination of prophetic leading and circumstances. The church was able to develop the strategy and put significant resources into the work—with long-term impacts in Ukraine. Many church members, along with other supporters, have been able to identify with this strategy and get behind it with finances, prayer, and other practical support over the years.

The local church can, and should, develop strategic goals in terms of its work on behalf of those in poverty. The early church, as described in Acts, provides some good examples. Let's look for a moment at the Jerusalem church in the period soon after the day of Pentecost. A social need emerged quite quickly. A number of widows were coming to faith and joining the Jerusalem church. However, they were poor, and many of them did not have their own jobs or any family to support them. No doubt individual church members were helping specific widows, but the church realised that this was such a major need that they required a strategy. So a programme of free food distribution was arranged for these widows and others in need. Then when this got a bit disorganised, seven capable men were appointed to lead and organise the food distribution to ensure that it was done systematically and fairly:

> In those days when the number of disciples was increasing, the Hellenistic Jews among them complained against the Hebraic Jews because their widows were being overlooked in the daily distribution of food. So the Twelve gathered all the disciples together and said, 'It would not be right for us to neglect the ministry of the word of God in order to wait on tables. Brothers and sisters, choose seven

men from among you who are known to be full of the Spirit and wisdom. We will turn this responsibility over to them and will give our attention to prayer and the ministry of the word.'

This proposal pleased the whole group. They chose Stephen, a man full of faith and of the Holy Spirit; also Philip, Procorus, Nicanor, Timon, Parmenas, and Nicolas from Antioch, a convert to Judaism. They presented these men to the apostles, who prayed and laid their hands on them. (Acts 6:1–6)

This is what I call strategy! As soon as this kind of strategy is in place, then church members are able to invest specifically in a shared social goal which the church has identified and acted upon.

Giving to those in need is often a spontaneous act of kindness. That is a wonderful thing. However, living a lifestyle that prioritises care for those in need requires more than spontaneous kindness—it involves strategy and planning. Some of that planning is about making financial resources available to be given away—as discussed above. This is a lifestyle choice. This is about choosing simplicity. But we also need to be strategic. Every individual disciple and every family needs to decide what longer-term strategic actions they can take to help those in poverty. What about sacrificial giving to church-based projects or charities? What about making time available to work with those living in poverty? What about making our homes available to those in need?

Let's be strategic!

From cynicism to expectancy

It has never been so easy to sit in the comfort of our own homes, with anonymity, and criticise others. Most of us can literally sit at home and watch the world go by through the eyes of television and social media. (Many of us had no choice but to do this during the coronavirus pandemic, but for some it has long been a habit outside of lockdown.) The amount of information at our fingertips is staggering. The opportunities to comment on what is happening in the world around us are unprecedented. This can be used very positively—but very often it isn't. The development of social media has led to mountains of unsolicited and random comment on almost everything that happens in life. It is so easy to criticise or condemn. It is so easy to 'like' negative opinions. Trolling and online abuse is a worldwide problem. It can be shocking to see what some people put up on social media.

This culture of increasing cynicism also affects social justice issues. While there are still some idealists and pragmatists out there, much of the narrative is negative.

What do you think when you hear of aid money being wasted through corruption? Of church leaders compromised by sexual double standards? Of charities paying oversized salaries to their senior staff? Of government welfare policies that seem to make life worse for those on benefits? Or of welfare benefits claimants discovered to be cheating the system? Such scandals are instantly given media prominence. They are sensational. They show up hypocrisy. They make us feel better about ourselves. They reinforce our love of being armchair critics. They provoke yet another social media storm of indignation.

Christians need to be very aware of this as a cultural trend which can easily overtake us and shape our outlooks. The risk is that we are shaped by the major emphasis on cynicism in this area rather than having a more godly response.

What could that response look like?

To start with, we should be wise enough to know that such human corruption is inevitable. We are realistic about human sinfulness. And yet, we are called to a life of faith.

Cynicism is the opposite of faith. Cynicism produces passivity; faith produces energetic activism. Cynicism tolerates injustice; faith challenges injustice. Cynicism creates a sense of detachment; faith leads to compassionate engagement. Our faith in God is a faith in divine power to change people's hearts and lives. Faith to believe that the church can really bring 'good news to the poor'.

Study Topics

1. Read Matthew 6:19–34. Discuss how this passage guides us on the road to 'simplicity'.

2. How has the 'complexity' of modern life affected you and your family/household? What can you specifically do to move from 'complexity' towards 'simplicity'?

3. What practical steps can we take as individuals to overcome the tendency to use money only to protect ourselves and create comfort for our families/households?

4. Think about the people you know and your friendships. What can you do practically to increase your engagement with people who are different from you and who face issues with poverty or social need?

5. Are you involved in a local church? If so, to what level? How important do you consider commitment to a local church to be for practical discipleship?

6. How strategic are you in using your finances and other resources to help people in poverty or need? How can you become more strategic? What steps will be needed?

7. How strategic is your church in using its resources to help people in poverty or need? Do you think it needs to become more strategic? If so, how can you encourage and advocate for change? What support might Jubilee+ provide?

8. Discuss the difference between 'cynicism' and 'expectancy'. Which of these two words best describes your approach to poverty and need?

9. How can you use social media to make a positive difference for those in poverty or who are vulnerable? How can your church do the same?

CHAPTER FOUR

POVERTY-BUSTING INCLUSIVITY

Out of the blue, I (Natalie) received a message from a woman in the church inviting me to a party she was throwing for a friend on a special occasion. A former drug addict from one of the roughest parts of town, she had become a Christian and been in the church for about ten years, but I had only recently started getting to know her. Her invitation came with a cautionary note: 'We will all be trolleyed [very drunk],' she wrote, 'so I'll understand if you don't want to come.'

When I turned up at her house, it was obvious that she hadn't been joking. I could hear the party as I drove into her street. As I walked around the side of her house and into the garden, guests were dancing, shrieking with laughter, and drinking.

When my friend spotted me, she came over and slurred into my ear: 'Thanks for coming. It means a lot. You're the only one from the church who's come.'

I got myself a drink—something homemade that tasted lethal, which I quickly replaced with something more socially acceptable for a Christian: lemonade. I went back to my friend, who really was 'trolleyed', and she told me, in her drunkenness, that God had told her not to pursue her career for the time being but instead to give a year of her life to volunteering with our church, specifically in the projects that care for those in poverty in our community, and to live by faith.

I was about to respond with something 'wise'—my gut instinct was to counsel her against doing this, as she's a single parent raising and supporting her children on her own. But before I had a chance, she said: 'So I've done it.'

I was shocked. 'What do you mean?' I asked.

'Well, God told me to do it so I've done it,' she said.

A couple of things quickly struck me about this. First of all, it's really easy to look at my friend in judgement. Some of us might be tempted to think she's not quite grasped the gospel because she's been a Christian for years and here she is, still getting drunk and seeming not to be bothered about it or think it's a problem. The Bible tells us clearly not to get drunk, but to instead be filled with the Spirit. Many of us who have been Christians for a while may find it pretty easy not to drink to excess.

If I look at my friend at this party and then look at me with my lemonade, I could very easily fall into the trap of thinking about how well I'm doing because outwardly I have the appearance of a good Christian.

But I know full well that if God asked me to give up my job for a year I'd say no several times before I'd obey. He would have to coerce and coax me into obedience. But this friend of mine obeyed immediately! Whatever is going on outwardly, her heart to do as God says as soon as she hears him say it is in a different league to my own. Jesus said that if we love him we'll obey him. I easily avoid getting drunk, but sometimes I struggle to give God even an hour of my day. Yet here's my friend drunk, yes, but radically obeying God the moment she hears him speak and giving him a year of her life to do what he wants her to.

If she'd asked my advice, rather than telling me when it was a done deal, I'd have cautioned her to be wise. I'd have said, 'Come on, you've got kids, you need to be sensible.' And I would've stood in the way of everything God has wanted to do in her life in the year she gave to him. She has so many stories of God's miraculous provision, of hearing his voice, and spent much of her year lifting others out of poverty. She became a vital link between people in the poorest parts of our community who were new Christians, and the church. She spent her year doing what Isaiah 61 says—rebuilding, renewing, and restoring others—in a way that the majority of people in my mostly middle-class church couldn't, at least not so naturally.

If I'm honest, when she first told me she wanted to volunteer for the church, one of my thoughts was: 'I'll spend some time with her, come alongside her, help her grow as a Christian, disciple her, and maybe have an opportunity to shape her.'

What happened was pretty much the opposite. I learnt so much about what it means to humbly, radically obey Jesus, to serve others and lift them up when it's unseen, when no one knows, when it can't be used as a story or an illustration in a talk or a book, but is just about your own walk with God.

I got to see my friend sacrificially love others and serve them, and I saw the power of that in their lives and hers, but I also saw the power of it in my own life as it provoked me.

It's really easy for us, if we've been Christians for any length of time and outwardly look like we've got ourselves all sorted, to miss how thoroughly Jesus wants our hearts and our unequivocal obedience. I know that left to my own devices, without the work of the Holy Spirit in my life, I want to be just radical enough that I can feel good about myself—just radical enough that others are a little bit impressed with me—but not so radical that it's truly costly or causes me any pain or discomfort.

As I watched my friend live out Isaiah 61 and act like Jesus, it made me love him more and want to be more like him. And I think that's exactly the point—Jesus invites us to be like him, to lay down our lives, and to be servants of all. When we do, others are drawn to him. Some want to know him, and some who already know him see such beauty in us—in the way we show his mercy to others and sacrifice our comfort, letting him have everything he wants, for his glory and for the good of those around us—that they want to be more and more like him too!

But this can only happen when we're willing to lay down our preconceived ideas, examine ourselves soberly to discover our prejudices, and recognise that we all have something to learn from those from different backgrounds, walks of life, and experiences. Often, it's the very people we feel superior to whom God is bringing alongside us, not so we can change *their* attitudes and actions, but so that he can shape *our* hearts and behaviour through them. The more time I spend with people I want to help, the more God works on, in, and through me.

God is calling his people to be an army of mercy-bringers that looks radically different to the world. Not for the sake of being radical, not so we can feel good about how radical we are, but so that we can point our hurting, fractured, divided communities to Jesus as the one who values what the world considers worthless, rushes in to bind up what is broken, and raises up those others would push aside.

The long road of sanctification

The purpose of telling the story of my friend was not to cause a debate about drunkenness and outward sin versus the hidden attitudes of our hearts, which it could easily start. Although valid, that's for another place. Rather, it is an illustration to challenge us to look deeper: I have lost count of the number of times I have quoted 'God looks at the heart' (1 Sam. 16:7) but then a second later carried on looking at the very things the world looks at! I wonder if you're like me …

The point of the story about my friend is also to challenge us not to fall into the trap of our modern world, where we want things now—quick fixes, everything at the touch of a button—that can lead us to want even our sanctification in an instant. Discipleship is a long journey. It's a really, really long road. God is astonishingly patient with us, and we need to be far more patient with those we walk alongside. God is often doing a deep work in someone's life, but if we're only looking at what's on the surface, we might miss it.

Over the year that my friend spent volunteering, I had the privilege of seeing her grow in both character and gifting. A few months into it, she said to me one day: 'God has spoken to me about drinking too much. I need to put in place things that help me avoid it.' This made me laugh to myself about how easily I forget that the Holy Spirit is very good at what he does! We get the privilege of walking alongside people, supporting them, encouraging them, picking them up on things, and having them do the same for us. But none of us can do the job of the Holy Spirit, which is to genuinely change hearts.

The world-famous twentieth-century evangelist Billy Graham said this: 'It's the Holy Spirit's job to convict, God's job to judge, and my job to love.' How often I get my job wrong, trying to take a role that wasn't designed for me! And when we try to do the Spirit's job for him, we can only achieve the poor substitute of behaviour modification.

That is actually part of my own story too. I became a Christian when I was fifteen years old. I didn't grow up in a Christian family. I grew up in one of the most deprived parts of the UK. A national newspaper called the *Daily Mail* once wrote a headline about my hometown, Hastings, calling it 'Hell-on-Sea'!

When I was really small, we lived in a council flat on the sixteenth floor. We had no central heating, and the only phone was a communal one on the ground floor. My parents' income was so low that I qualified for free school meals—I was one of only two people in my class at primary school who was given a free hot meal every lunchtime. By the UK government's definition of poverty at the time, I grew up in a working-class family that was in relative poverty.[1]

I wasn't overly aware of it as a young child, but I became more aware of it once I became a Christian—not necessarily that my family didn't have as much as others, but that we had a different way of doing certain things.

For example, going to other people's houses for dinner was a cause of great anxiety for me because, before I became a Christian, I'd never seen food served in different dishes for different types of food—meat in one dish, vegetables in another, potatoes in another, and so on.

But once I became a Christian, people invited me over for dinner and they'd serve food up like this, and then they'd say that I should go first because I was the guest. I would feel really anxious about it because I had no idea if you were supposed to start with one type of food or another, or how much you should take to look like you were grateful but not greedy.

I also tried to change the way I talk. Though I am a stickler for correct spelling and grammar when I write, multiple letters are dropped from words when I speak. Without thinking about it, I even tend to say my own name as 'Na-er-lie' or 'Nat-lie'! I have joked occasionally about 'my posh voice', which I seem to adopt unconsciously when speaking to people who I think will judge me based on how I talk. You might think that doesn't happen in Christian circles, but some people have been honest enough to tell me about assumptions they made about me when they heard me speak. One church leader who interviewed me for a training course later told someone he nearly fell off his chair when I mentioned I was about to start studying for my master's degree in political communications.

I have had to change some things about the way I speak since becoming a Christian. For example, I rarely swear these days, I avoid lying, and I don't engage in coarse joking. All of these have been part of my discipleship as a follower of Jesus. But what I've realised in the last few years is that following Jesus doesn't mean I have to sound middle-class. And since I grasped that, I have started to drop my posh accent (it wasn't actually posh anyway!) and re-adopt my natural way of speaking. I'm now embracing the way I sound because I've understood that it doesn't need to change.

These are just two examples of many I could tell you about how I spent the first twenty years of my Christian life learning to behave like the people around me rather than like Jesus Christ. I started to become middle-class, not because I wanted or intended to, but because I mistook middle-class behaviour for Christ-like behaviour. I learnt quickly to outwardly conform to the behaviour of the people around me, often feeling very at odds with it, but not realising for years that God has saved me because of my background, not despite it.

Please don't misunderstand me—there's nothing wrong with being middle-class. But it's not the goal of discipleship. On reflection now, I very much doubt God has ever cared about whether I know which fork to eat with or that I'm supposed to take a bottle of wine to someone's house if they invite me for a meal.

God's concern is that I become like Jesus!

What he saved me for wasn't so I could learn how to behave like all of the middle-class Christians around me. That's not his heart for me, and it wasn't his heart for my friend. His vision for us has always been that we would be rebuilders of ancient ruins, renewers of those around us, and restorers of long-devastated places—places that some would label 'Hell-on-Sea'.

According to Isaiah 61, that's the vision that God has for people trapped in poverty when he saves them. The good news that came to me when I was in poverty wasn't that I might eat nice dinners at people's houses, go to university, acquire some wealth, and make for myself a nice comfortable middle-class life.

No! The good news that Jesus brought to me was that the Creator of the universe knows my name and has chosen me to be his daughter, part of his family. He's not ashamed of me or embarrassed by me. He delights in me, sings over me, and calls me his own.

Becoming oaks of righteousness

A while back I asked my youth leaders from when I got saved what I was like back then. They said: 'You were a right screwed-up mess!'

I was trouble, and I was troubled. But my background and how messed up I was—the fact that I didn't know how to behave like the nice Christians I met at church—this was no obstacle to God saving me. In fact, if we look at 1 Corinthians 1 where it says that 'God chose what is foolish in the world to shame the wise; God chose what is weak in the world to shame the strong; God chose what is low and despised in the world, even the things that are not ...' then we see that, if anything, my background is *why* he saved me!

With this in mind, it is so important that we create inclusive churches where we don't try to mould people from different backgrounds to our likeness. We should seek to enable them to conform to the image of Christ in a way that doesn't pull them away from their lives, experiences, neighbourhoods, and social settings. We should equip them to flourish in a distinctive way that reflects where they have come from.

God chooses those we write off. He looks at the people that society has no hope for, no regard for, no interest in, and he longs for us. Jesus told us that the kingdom of God belongs to the poor, and James reminds us that God has chosen the poor to be rich in faith (2:5).

Yet somehow, in the church, we often lean towards mimicking society rather than imitating God when we look at impressive people and think, 'They would make a good Christian.' When we are drawn to the people who have influential careers, lots of money, great intellect, grand social status—we are not being drawn to the people Jesus spent most of his time with. In fact, James writes that when we prioritise people according to their wealth or status, we have 'become judges with evil thoughts' (2:4). If we know that we have a tendency to value the outward things that the world values, this verse should arrest our hearts and propel us into sober assessment. It's not that we condemn ourselves, but that we allow the Word of God to convict us and recalibrate our attitudes to align with his.

Unity in diversity

So how do we build poverty-busting inclusive church communities? Ones where people from all walks of life can sit side by side, worshipping God together, serving alongside one another, spurring one another on to good works, and encouraging each other to become more like Jesus?

It starts with understanding that the church is supposed to be beautifully diverse: we are supposed to come from hugely varied backgrounds but be united in Christ, a demonstration to the world around us that God is real and he is good and when he touches our hearts, barriers between us are stripped away as we become brothers and sisters, joined together by the blood of Jesus.

However, as Ben Lindsay points out in his book *We Need to Talk About Race*,[2] diversity on its own is not sufficient—it is entirely possible for our churches to have diversity without inclusivity. They are actually fundamentally different. As Martin and I wrote in *A Church for the Poor*, diversity and segregation can coexist in the same Sunday church meeting and in the same small group and so on: 'Some of us are in diverse churches but never mix with those in the congregation who are from different backgrounds.'[3]

Race is a vital issue when it comes to creating inclusive churches that see people lifted up out of poverty because you are more likely to grow up in poverty in the Western world if you are not white. For example, in the UK white British people are the least likely to live in the most deprived neighbourhoods in the country,[4] while 45 percent of children in ethnic minority families live in poverty (compared with 26 percent of white British children).[5] This continues into adulthood, with black and other minority ethnic workers far more likely to be in insecure work—one in twenty-four are on zero-hour contracts (compared to one in forty-two white workers), and they are twice as likely to be stuck on agency contracts and report not having enough hours to make ends meet.[6] The coronavirus pandemic drew this inequality into sharp focus too, with COVID-19 deaths among people of black African heritage living in England and Wales three times the rate of white Britons. In fact, 'the head of NHS England advised [that medical] staff from black, Asian and ethnic minority groups should be "risk-assessed" as a precaution based on the growing data'.[7] If we want our churches to be inclusive in a way that tackles poverty and supports people out of it, then we need to be reaching out to those most affected by poverty.

Once we understand that God's plan has always been to have a diverse group of people to call his own, and that there are supposed to be no dividing walls of hostility within this group, then we start to realise two crucial things. One is that we need to surrender our tribalism while at the same time retaining our diversity. We are not supposed to be identical—God wants a diverse family of followers, not a group of clones. God doesn't want to transform us beyond recognition from who we were and what we had experienced before he rescued us. Rather, he wants to redeem it all, drawing out all the ways in which we bear his image. He wants us to take on all the characteristics of Christ—gentleness, wisdom, love, joy, righteousness, peace, self-control, etc.—but to then reflect him to those around us in the unique way that he has designed us and planned for us to do. When we come together as the church, then together we display God's glory, wisdom, and pre-eminence.

Flourishing where God has placed us

Related to this, the second vital truth we realise is that we're not to try to nudge disciples increasingly away from their histories, their personalities, or their communities. Upward mobility is not the goal of the gospel. Neither is behaviour modification. God doesn't extract us from the people around us when we're saved. He's planted us there! We have been saved for a purpose: to be conformed to the image of Jesus (Rom. 8:28–29) and to love our neighbours.

If everyone who gets saved in your church ends up moving into the same neighbourhood, sending their kids to the same schools, shopping in the same small area of the community, then who will reach the parts of the town or city left behind? Jesus said we're to look for men (and women) of peace wherever we go (Luke 10:6). We are not to avoid or shun certain neighbourhoods. We are to look for people of peace within them, introduce them to Jesus, and then support them as they seek, empowered by the Holy Spirit, to transform the locality around them by advancing the kingdom. How might this look? Perhaps it would look like crime rates falling, drug dealing and violence becoming rare, neighbours who previously didn't get on now being reconciled and caring for one another. Kingdom flourishing means hearts and lives transformed, not necessarily bank balances boosted.

There is also a practical concern here: reaching out across classes and social divides is, in reality, cross-cultural mission, which is hard. That doesn't mean we shouldn't do it, but it does mean we should recognise that when someone with a particular background or life experience is saved, they are going to be able to tell their peers about Jesus in a much more natural and easy way than an 'outsider'.

We can and should be committed to cross-cultural mission and to churches that reflect the beautiful diversity mentioned above, but the reality is that many of us will struggle to connect with those whose lives have nothing in common with ours. Of course, once someone has come to know Jesus, we're absolutely to make every effort to break down walls and love each other. The Bible is clear—we're to bear with, honour, spur on, and love one another—including those whom we would naturally have no time for if we weren't united in Christ. In fact, especially those, because we are all called to hospitality and love that transcend the things that would, outside of Christ, divide us. But before someone responds to the gospel, overcoming the walls we all put up to safeguard our way of life is very hard indeed.

In Christ, it's not impossible. Some are specifically called to this, and all of us should reach out to whomever we can, whenever we can, in whatever ways we can. However, it's important to remember that God has called each one of us to 'our people'—our families, friends, neighbours, and work colleagues—placing us deliberately alongside the people we know and love that they might come to know Jesus and join 'his people'. And only then is the wonderful, wall-shattering glory of God's family displayed.

It is vital we reach people 'like us', and we must break down barriers. It is not one or the other.

All churches start in a specific social context, such as on an estate, in middle-class suburbia, in an inner city, or in a remote village. There is nothing wrong with this, but when it comes to local churches, we must not entrench in one specific culture but seek to diversify over time if we're to truly reflect the gospel. This requires intentional engagement with other social groups. We explored in our previous book various strategies for this.[8] This kind of unity in diversity involves us to consider the main culture and the various subcultures that exist among our congregations—again, something we wrote about in detail in *A Church for the Poor*.[9] When we have diversity among groups who would usually be divided, it's a powerful witness to the gospel of Jesus.

While we categorically want to see every disciple raised up out of their poverty and flourishing in their local church context, this will look very different from person to person. My sanctification journey, as someone saved out of relative poverty, from a working-class background, a broken family, supported by the State's welfare system, will look very different to the journey of my co-author, who grew up in a secure middle-class family, attended a private boarding school, and travelled to different continents throughout his childhood.

Both of us are called to increasingly become like Jesus. Neither of us is called to increasingly become like the other. We make this mistake to the detriment of our churches, because it is incredibly powerful when people from such starkly contrasting backgrounds demonstrate the gospel at work through their unity in Christ. This is one of the reasons Martin and I write together. We are such unlikely co-authors, yet our very different life experiences, personalities, and walks with God have led us to a shared conviction that God is profoundly and uncompromisingly concerned about those facing poverty and injustice in the world and calls Christians to share that concern and act upon it.

This goes beyond social status, wealth, and class. Recent research in the UK has indicated that one of the key factors in children who grow up in the church and continue in their faith into adulthood is an older non-family member coming alongside them in their teens and twenties. Inter-generational relationships make a difference.[10] We need to not only celebrate diversity, but look to create an inclusivity that actively encourages church members to be friends with people who are not like them.

Not only are our churches impoverished when some people are inadvertently forced to conform, or feel excluded if they don't, but poverty itself is accentuated if there is no place for particular types of people in the church.

So what are we to do?

The first question is this: are you mixing—meaningfully—with people who are not like you? Do you have friends whose behaviour sometimes makes you wince? Whom you don't always understand? Whose attitudes to family, health, money, food, socialising, and so on are very different to yours? If we really want to live lifestyles that are inclusive towards those who have less than us (or more than us, for that matter), then it has to start with who we're personally friends with.

This isn't just about who we'll speak to over a cup of coffee after our Sunday morning meetings or interact with during other church activities. It is about whom we share our lives with. I am a single woman and live on my own. Meals have become the primary way in which I experience church as family. There are several people in my church who frequently feed me. In fact, in 2019 I managed to go forty-six consecutive days without needing to turn on my oven: I ate with friends for a month and an half. Often, I invited myself to their houses. There are a small number of families in the church who never seem to tire of my company—they seem happy to have me over for dinner as often as I like. These families don't treat me like a guest when I arrive. They don't bring out their fancy china. They don't set the table with candelabra and engraved cutlery. No! What makes these dinner tables feel like home to me is that I'm treated like one of the family. This means that sometimes I walk into someone's home and they say, 'Would you like a cup of tea?' and when I say, 'Yes,' they respond with, 'Great, put the kettle on and make one for me as well, please!' Ironically, we actually find family when we're *not* being treated as if we're special.

Through eating with friends in the church, the church has become my family. What's more, God has powerfully communicated his love and affection for me through the homes where I feel at home. Please don't underestimate the impact a simple invitation to dinner can have on someone different to you. Regular time with those who are different to me—whether richer or poorer—has enriched my life, my faith, and my understanding of God. Jesus ate with a wide variety of people—usually on their territory. He was happy to eat with people whom others wouldn't even speak with. Jesus ate with tax collectors and 'sinners'—this included prostitutes, thieves, and gamblers. He ate with a man everyone else avoided, known as 'Simon the Leper' (would we?!), and he ate with a supposedly morally upright religious leader, Simon the Pharisee. Jesus ate with the rich and he ate with the poor. He fed the crowds and he picked out a short man called Zacchaeus. He ate with those who would deny him and with one who would betray him. He ate with those who wished him harm and with those who loved him. He ate with the oppressed and—perhaps even more shockingly for some of us activists—with the oppressor!

It's not enough to give food to those in poverty through our food-banks or soup kitchens or feeding programmes. I have heard Jackie Pullinger say, 'Don't just give people the church's food. Give them yours!' If we say we have a heart for those in poverty but wouldn't contemplate inviting the people we're helping to eat at our own dinner tables, it is well worth stopping to ponder what's really going on within us.

In Luke's gospel we read what Jesus has to say about who we should invite for dinner:

> When you give a dinner or a banquet, do not invite
> your friends or your brothers or your relatives or
> your rich neighbours, lest they also invite you in

return and you be repaid. But when you give a feast, invite the poor, the crippled, the lame, the blind, and you will be blessed, because they cannot repay you. For you will be repaid at the resurrection of the just. (Luke 14:12–14 ESV)

Later in that same chapter we see that when we do this, we reflect the kingdom of God, where Jesus says that many who were invited didn't want to come, and so the Great Banquet is filled with the poor and sick, those who would never usually be invited.

In *The Message* Bible, the words of Jesus in Luke 14 are paraphrased as this: 'Don't just invite … the kind of people who will return the favor. Invite some people who never get invited out, the misfits from the wrong side of the tracks.'

Setting a place at your dinner table—especially for someone whose life looks very different from yours or whom society wouldn't expect you to mix with—is a powerful act of inclusion. Whether it's someone from a different tribe or from another part of your town or city, someone with a job that others find offensive or with bad hygiene or ill health, those with mental health issues or addictions, someone who is just as likely to steal from you as to eat with you—when we eat with people who are 'not like us', our hospitality is powerful.

Some of us may even be challenged to go further: a friend recently talked to me about his family's journey into fostering, saying that he had talked to his children about 'giving our family as a gift to someone' who needs it. Across the UK, people are opening their homes to unaccompanied child refugees and adult survivors of modern slavery. The charity Home for Good (homeforgood.org.uk) is at the forefront of urging Christians to see their families as a safe place for the thousands of children in the care system who need secure homes.

We must stop treating our homes as our castles and instead acknowledge that where we live is a gift from God, not meant for our exclusive use but for the inclusion of others. This is also true of our money, which, like our homes, is another area of our lives on which we can be prone to hold a vice-like grip. But it's not ours. It comes from God and belongs to him.

It is fascinating that when God was setting out how his people Israel should live—the Law they were to follow that would cause them to thrive and be distinctive from every nation around them, so that all would marvel and ultimately recognise that they followed the one true God—he said that there need not be anyone in poverty among them. 'There need be no poor people among you, for in the land the LORD your God is giving you to possess as your inheritance, he will richly bless you, if only you fully obey the LORD your God and are careful to follow all these commandments I am giving you today' (Deut. 15:4–5).

However, the people of God didn't obey him, they didn't follow his commandments, and so there were people in need in their midst. But then we come to the book of Acts, where we see the early church in action. Jesus has died, been resurrected, and has ascended. The Holy Spirit has come and now we find that followers of Jesus, full of the power of the Holy Spirit, are able to live as God intended. What's the outworking of this? The fulfilment of Deuteronomy 15!

All the believers were one in heart and mind. No
one claimed that any of their possessions was their

own, but they shared everything they had … And God's grace was so powerfully at work in them all that *there was no needy person among them.* For from time to time those who owned land or houses sold them, brought the money from the sales and put it at the apostles' feet, and it was distributed to anyone who had need. (Acts 4:32–35, emphasis added)

Whether it's our homes, our dinner tables, or our money, what we have is not our own and is not solely for us. Whatever God has given us, it is for his glory and for the good of those around us. If we want to build inclusive churches, we need to have a far more radical approach to our belongings. And we need a far more radical approach to our attitudes. We need to be willing to surrender our ways of thinking, as well as our wallets, to God.

On a church level, what proportion of our income is spent on helping people in poverty? Often when we look at offerings in the Bible—whether in the Old Testament Law or in the New Testament book of Acts and the Epistles—we see that they weren't solely about funding or supporting leaders, but about ensuring there was no one in need. Individually, too, God is after our money! He wants us to have the right perspective on our money, which is that it is his and not ours. This means when someone in your church community tells you they are in need, your first response might not be to pray for them but to answer the prayer you would have prayed!

I recently had an opportunity to put this into practice. Someone in the church was telling me about their credit card debt. They were only paying off the interest and couldn't make any headway with the actual debt itself. As they spoke to me, I was thinking that I would offer to pray for them. But God told me to lend them the money interest-free, as in the Law of Moses. I said, 'No.' I didn't want to do that. But out of interest I asked the person how much their debt was. Now I love a story about someone needing a very specific amount of money, and that exact amount coming through the letterbox. But to be honest, I was far less happy when the person told me the amount they needed to clear their credit card debt was very close to the amount I had sitting in a bank account, ready in case anything went wrong with my home or car. I knew God was speaking to me, yet still I resisted. I often speak on the beauty of the Sabbath Year in the Old Testament, when debts were cancelled, and how wonderful it is that God said no interest should be charged on loans. But I didn't want to do what he was asking me to do. I didn't want to put my money where my mouth is. In the end, though, after several minutes of wrestling with God in my head, I felt him nudge me with this: 'It isn't your money, though.'

How could I argue with that? Reluctantly, I offered to lend the person the money interest-free. At that point their eyes welled up and they told me they had been ashamed of their debt, not wanting to tell anyone, but the fact that the first person they told had acted with kindness towards them had revealed to them that God was on their side and wanted them to be free.

It was an amazing moment that taught me a lot. God wants access to everything we have. If we are those who run projects and push our churches further into God's heart for those in poverty, this must be backed up by the way we live our own lives too. Full, poverty-busting inclusivity says, 'What's mine isn't just mine. It's yours too.' It is radically counter-cultural to a Western mind-set.

Likewise, God wants access to our attitudes. Are we open to changing our minds about people-groups and individuals? So often we remain stubbornly committed to our way of thinking, even when it sets us apart from other people. God wants us to approach everyone we meet—both inside and outside the church—with the knowledge that they are made in his image and precious to him. That's true of every single person. If we cannot see the image of God in someone, the problem is not with them but with us.

What if it's their own fault?

Whether a person got themselves into the mess they're in or is a victim of circumstances, God's response is to be merciful towards them. Psalm 107 offers an interesting perspective on this. In it we read of four groups of people:

- those wandering in the desert, hungry and thirsty (vv. 4–5);
- those in darkness and chains because they had rebelled against God and ignored his wisdom (vv. 10–11);
- those who were foolish and suffering because of their own sins (v. 17);
- and those who went out in ships to do business and make a living, who got into peril in a storm and were at their wits' end (vv. 23–27).

Two of these groups are clearly in trouble and distress because of their own actions, but the wanderers and the sailors don't seem to have done anything wrong. Four groups of people with four different sets of circumstances, but the one thing they have in common is that they cry out to God in their distress. And guess what? God answers them all in the same way—he delivers them all. He shows them mercy not because they deserve it but because he's merciful and his heart is for those he has made.

He invites us to be like him in this—to show mercy where others would run dry, to see people how he sees them, and to have compassion on them. Building an inclusive church begins with a sober assessment of ourselves—recognising the relentless mercy that we have required day by day—and then a surrendering of our attitudes to God, that we might see people as he sees them.

Building bridges, not walls

We live in a time of astonishing connectivity. Whether you're in Singapore or Seattle, South Africa or Southend, chances are you're living your life in public to one degree or another through social media. So one of the major ways in which we need to submit our attitudes to God is through our online discourse. While writing this book, I've seen Christians tear each other to shreds on social media over points of doctrine, and I've seen the same happen over behaviour in everyday life. One professing Christian challenged another to encourage a political leader to 'throw herself out of a window', while another wrote that there's no place for being friendly in politics. All of this is sinful. We are to conduct ourselves in a manner worthy of the calling we've received (cf. Eph. 4:1; Col. 1:10; Rom. 12)! This means online as well as offline. Jesus is calling us to be far more thoughtful with what we post online than those around us. Christians should be setting an example in building bridges, not walls. We can express an opinion, even a strong one, but we need to do so in a way that leaves the other person intact, doesn't tear down but honours, disagrees well, doesn't resort to tribal factions but instead seeks to understand people of different opinions, values, and beliefs.

God wants us to express his heart for those in need. He calls us to imitate Jesus in all areas of life, which includes caring about those whom no one else cares about. If we take this seriously, it will make us extremely uncomfortable. It means giving God full access to what we own, what we say, where we live, and whom we're friends with.

If we want to live in a way that truly demonstrates God's heart for the poorest among us and around us, we must start with *our own* hearts, minds, and behaviours. When we do, we display the power and beauty of the gospel—and of God—in bringing together (in a fully inclusive way) those whom society would keep apart. This is the church.

There's a lot for us to do collectively, too. Many of us will be in the majority culture in our churches, even if we weren't originally. Though I felt very different from those around me in church when I was first saved, it's now more than two decades on and I can do a pretty good job of looking like everyone around me, even when I feel I don't fit. I have learnt how to behave, and now much of it comes naturally to me. I've become part of the dominant culture in the church. The onus has to be on those of us in the majority to make space for those in the minority, or in subcultures within the church. We explored this concept in our previous book.[11]

A good starting place for the church is to ask those from minority cultures—whether that's class, age, race, etc.—what they like about various church activities and what they find hard. Open and honest dialogue is a key to integration. Trying to think through how you might inadvertently exclude, alienate, or even offend other people is important. For example, if you have people in your Sunday meetings who cannot read or for whom English is their second language, how can you help them to be fully included in everything you do? This might be as simple as playing new songs for twenty minutes before the meeting starts so that those who cannot read can learn the words by hearing them.

Perhaps the thing that will make the most difference is having people from different backgrounds on our leadership teams, in our worship bands, and as small-group leaders. Do you have people in these positions who have lived or are living in poverty? This is not about tokenism, but it is about affirmative action. Those in the majority culture need to take responsibility for drawing out the skills, giftings, and abilities of those in the minority subcultures in your congregation. Someone's leadership style may not look like yours, but that doesn't mean they can't lead. You might find you have a lot to learn from how someone from a poorer background handles responsibility and pastoral care!

If we are really serious about inclusivity of people from all backgrounds in our churches, it will affect each area of church life. We will need to think through our preaching (content and length!), worship, spiritual gifts, youth and children's groups, mid-week groups, the coffee we serve, the expectations we place on people. I recently hosted a small-group meeting where everyone was invited to bring snacks or drinks to share. Someone turned up with two big bags of crisps—both half empty. But that's ok, isn't it? It might not be the 'done thing', but why shouldn't it be? If we ask people to bring snacks or drinks, we need to get over our own standards of what is acceptable and what isn't.

In order to help people find real community among us, in a lasting way, we need to think through what we might be doing that is unhelpful, and what we can do differently in order to make it easier for people to fully integrate and become part of us. Undoubtedly, this will often require teaching the church to interact meaningfully with people who may have completely different backgrounds and life experiences. But it is well worth the time and effort to work towards being a church that truly reflects the diverse range of followers of Jesus.

Study Topics

1. How do we ensure we are aware of our attitudes and prejudices towards others? What can we do to challenge our own attitudes? Are we open to changing our minds about individuals/groups of people? Are we as open to changing our minds about the rich and powerful as we are about those in poverty?

2. Who are you inviting into your home?

3. Are you mixing—meaningfully—with people who are not like you, with different backgrounds, life experiences, and attitudes? How is this challenging you? How is it enriching you?

4. Can you think of examples of when God has taught you something through someone you were hoping to help or disciple?

5. Do you recognise in yourself a desire to be 'just radical enough that others are a little bit impressed ... but not so radical that it's truly costly, or causes any pain or discomfort'?

6. Can you think of times when you have modified your behaviour to fit in with those around you in church, or when you have wanted someone else to change their behaviour to become more like you, rather than more like Jesus?

7. As individual Christians and as church communities, is the way we spend our money truly reflecting our hearts for those in poverty?

CHAPTER FIVE

CHANGING YOUR COMMUNITY

The factor that has arguably the biggest impact on the lives of those facing poverty is how the State operates. Therefore it should be of fundamental importance to the church. If we want to see people raised out of poverty and the cords of injustice loosened (Isa. 58:6), we need to engage with the decision makers around us. So we need to cultivate a godly attitude towards those in power as well as those in poverty. Many of us are meeting people's needs at the point of crisis—whether it be a short, acute crisis or that their lives are perpetually in crisis. This is good and right, but if we do only this, we will end up supporting flawed (at best) or corrupt (at worst) structures and systems that continually push people into poverty or hold them down in it.

As Christians, we need to develop a two-pronged approach. Many of us find it easier to support people in need. On the one hand, this is vitally important and must not be neglected—Jesus often met people's immediate needs first, sometimes (as far as we know) never meeting their deepest need. Our work on the frontlines of poverty is crucial. Even in some of the richest countries on the planet, churches and Christians are literally saving lives through our social action projects. However, we run the risk of not only facilitating harmful State systems, but also creating dependency among those we long to help. Even when we don't want this to happen, it's easy to fall into the pattern of giving a handout rather than a hand up.

Spend just a few weeks talking to people living in poverty or facing injustice, and you are likely to quickly feel frustrated with the limited ways in which we help. We need a second string to our bow: we must lobby for structural and systemic changes in our cities and countries. We must 'speak up for those who cannot speak for themselves, for the rights of all who are destitute. Speak up and judge fairly; defend the rights of the poor and needy' (Prov. 31:8–9).

A seat at the table

For seven years, I (Natalie) ran communications for a local partnership of the police, government, healthcare, fire, probation, and other services. These frontline organisations worked together with the common goal of making our local community safer. The partnership achieved a high level of success in many areas; car crime and burglary, for example, fell dramatically for several years in a row. Our communications work to tackle the fear of crime—to make people aware that they were safer—won national and regional government recognition.

But there were some types of crime, such as violent crime in a public place, which we consistently seemed unable to reduce. The partnership board tried one tactic after another, and even though they didn't achieve the desired reductions, the next year they would decide to try the same again. Sometimes this was due to a lack of resources rather than a lack of ideas, but it always struck me that there wasn't any discussion of whether any churches or faith groups might have something to offer.

As a Christian, I found this frustrating. It didn't seem to even occur to the official agencies that the church might have any ideas or resources to contribute. Equally, the church hadn't positioned itself in such a way as to demonstrate that it might have innovative solutions to deep-seated, long-lasting problems. We weren't seen as those who 'restore the places long devastated' (Isa. 61:4) because, quite simply, we weren't engaging in any meaningful way with those making decisions that affected our local area.

Towards the end of my time at the partnership, this began to change on both counts. Firstly, I was asked twice to approach local church leaders to see if they could help with specific issues. Both times, the church leaders asked if they would be able to preach the gospel while helping. I explained that they could if asked what motivated them, but aside from that, it probably wouldn't be appropriate. Both times, in response to that, the church leaders declined the opportunity to get involved. This was a missed opportunity to build relationships, bless the work of others, and become justice- and hope-bringers to the community, as I'll demonstrate in a moment with the story of how my church has worked with the police and others to tackle human trafficking and modern slavery.

Secondly, the global financial crash happened in 2008, and people across the world who had previously been 'just about managing' were now squeezed hard and in some cases pushed into poverty. Communities were rocked. Churches started to realise they could and should help. They launched projects, and then more projects, and began to rediscover that concern for those in poverty, the oppressed, the marginalised, and the vulnerable is not peripheral to the gospel of Jesus Christ, but is central.

Suddenly the church, particularly in the Western world, began to wake up and recapture a Spirit-led compulsion to care for those in poverty. We longed for the days when people used to know they could knock on a church door and, even if everyone else had turned them away, here they would find new and enduring mercy and compassion. In my own town, first came Street Pastors—men and women who volunteered to go out into the town centre later at night on Fridays and Saturdays to help those who were vulnerable, often through intoxication. Police noticed that situations that would usually escalate into drink- or drug-fuelled violence were now being diffused by the mere presence of these Christians on the streets. Simple acts—such as giving lollipops to rowdy men leaving nightclubs and flip-flops to drunk women who could no longer walk in their heels—brought increasing peace to the town centre. Occasionally, there would be opportunities to pray with people right there on the streets in the early hours of the morning. One church began to open its doors late at night so that people could come in to find a hot drink, solace, or a friendly ear to listen to their woes.

When the church gets involved

Many Christians were challenged and inspired by a profound question often asked by British church leader David Carr: 'If your church closed its doors today, how long would it take your community to notice?'

Projects began to spring up, first in their ones and twos, then in their dozens, until churches in the UK were running well over four hundred foodbanks in one network alone (the Trussell Trust), and scores of church-run debt centres, night shelters, soup kitchens, and much more. Note that this was happening in one of the richest nations in the world.

Against this backdrop, a friend in my church had an image from God of a young woman from another country, beautiful but dishevelled and distressed. As my friend reflected on this image, over time she understood this woman to be a victim of human trafficking/ modern slavery. She started to pray more about this, drawing in a couple of others (including me) as we sought God for how we could help victims in our local area in some way.

By now I was working for my local church and asked my senior pastor if I could speak with the police on behalf of the church. It became clear that our local police didn't think prostitution and human trafficking were significant issues in our community. At the same time as this, our church had broadened the agenda of our prayer meetings, focusing increasingly on specific local issues, but praying in a different way. We continued to pray for revival, and for our members who were teachers, business leaders, etc. However, we now added in praying in more general terms for the common good, meaning we started praying for our hospital, whose maternity department was threatened with closure. We prayed for our schools, many of which were in 'special measures', meaning they were under-performing and deemed to need substantial improvement. And we prayed for our police.

We already had a few police officers in the church and when one of them told me that the most senior police officer in our town was coming to a prayer meeting, to be honest I was nervous. I thought she would find it strange, especially if we prayed in tongues! I worried about how some members of the church would interact with her. Midway through the meeting, the police chief asked if she could say something. She then told this small band of thirty to forty pray-ers that she was very surprised and grateful to find that we would pray for her and her officers in this way. She was visibly moved by her time with us and our evident care for her.

Still, the door to working with the police to tackle modern slavery and support victims seemed closed. Neither we nor the police chief could think of a way to work together, and from a policing perspective it wasn't a high priority because other crime types seemed more pressing.

Then a few weeks after this prayer meeting, I received a call from the police chief. She said, 'I've got a problem that no statutory agency can help me with. I wondered if the church might be able to help.' She told me about a victim of domestic abuse who had moved to Hastings after fleeing to a refuge. The perpetrator was about to be sentenced in a court that was 270 miles away, and the woman wanted to go to the court to see justice being done. But she didn't have any money and no official organisation had a budget to pay for something like this. 'Would the church pay for her train ticket, please? Is that the sort of thing a church does?' the police chief asked me.

While it certainly wasn't the 'sort of thing' we had done up until this point, thankfully I work for a church leader who is very open to doing things we haven't done before if he senses God at work. He said we could pay for the train ticket. When the survivor came to pick up the ticket, she asked if she had to come to church on Sunday. When we said she did not, she asked, 'What do I have to do?' We explained that she didn't need to do anything—that the ticket was a gift. She was overwhelmed. Obviously, we would never publicise something like this at the time, but later that day, the police chief tweeted: 'Thank you to King's Church for helping me with a problem that no one else was able to help me with.' We were amazed.

But still no door opened to help tackle modern slavery. The police chief moved on. Her successor was an officer I had clashed with in my previous job, so I thought that might be the end of the relationship that had started to form between the police and the church. However, the new police chief had heard about the train ticket purchased for the domestic abuse survivor, which led him to call asking for help with a very different situation.

He explained that there was a state-of-the-art skateboarding and BMX facility in our community that was never open to the public, but for one day local young people would be able to enjoy it as part of a twenty-four-hour 'skateathon' to raise money for local youth services facing funding cuts. The new police chief asked if my church could provide food at three different times during the 'skateathon'—sandwiches on the first evening, cereal and pastries for breakfast in the morning, and another round of sandwiches at lunchtime. The food wasn't actually for the young people taking part, but for the statutory agencies supporting the event—police officers, local councillors, fire officers, etc. He asked the same question as his predecessor: 'Is this the sort of thing a church can help with?'

Again, I wasn't sure that it was. It certainly didn't feel like 'core business' for a church. Yet God was clearly stirring something in our leadership team, and again our senior pastor gave the go-ahead. We put together three small teams, made enough food, not just for the authorities but for the young people too, and we determined to be as generous as possible. We supplied two rounds of sandwiches, cakes, and juices at the requested times, and our breakfast crew of two or three people really went above and beyond. As well as taking cereals and pastries, they took camping stoves and fried bacon and eggs for everyone finishing the night shift or starting on the early morning shift! When the police chief was quoted in the local newspaper about the event, much of what he said was in praise of the church's contribution.

Not long after this, we finally had an opportunity to help the police with modern slavery. They were planning a raid and needed a neutral venue to which they could bring any victims they rescued. They asked if they could use our church building, and of course we agreed as we were excited to finally be involved. The hours ticked by on that afternoon and no one came to us. A few hours after the raid, the police chief called to say that they hadn't rescued anyone, and we could 'stand down'. We were disappointed, but on the back of this I was invited into a multi-agency meeting to talk 'for five minutes' about human trafficking and modern slavery. I had attended many such meetings in my previous job, but this time, due to the sensitive information shared at the meeting, I would have to sign a confidentiality agreement and leave once I had spoken for my few minutes.

When I arrived, the police chief who had invited me wasn't there and no one seemed to know why I had been given a slot on the agenda. It was confusing for them to have someone from a church around the table. However, one of my previous bosses was there, so there was a friendly face. The chair of the meeting asked me to start, confirming that I'd need to leave after my five minutes. I started by saying, 'I know you're all aware that the Modern Slavery Bill is passing through Parliament and that you'll have increasing legislative responsibilities to tackle this crime when it becomes an Act, so I'm here on behalf of my church to offer to help you.' I spoke about the issue for my allotted five minutes. The chair thanked me, and I got up to leave. But my former boss asked me to wait, and then he addressed the representatives of various organisations in the room and vouched for me. Though he didn't use these words, he essentially said that I wasn't just some crazy Christian, but if I was offering to help, they should take me seriously.

The chair asked me to sit back down and said, 'Ok, how can you actually help us?' I was a little less prepared for this question, so I offered a lot of help that I had no idea how to actually deliver. They settled on training—they said they needed to know how to spot the signs of human trafficking, so would value our help with that. I said that the church would provide everything—venue, printed resources, a skilled trainer, refreshments, etc.—if they promised me they would bring twenty police officers along. They committed to that, and so the anti-trafficking work of King's Church in Hastings finally began.

My friend who had the vision of the distressed victim of modern slavery put the event together. She organised the majority of it, including booking an expert to deliver the training. When the day came to deliver it, instead of the twenty promised police officers, we had ninety-four people signed up for the event. This included the police, a large number of staff from our biggest housing association, fire officers, and staff from various departments of five local governments, even the man responsible for taxi licensing in the town. At the event we had the opportunity to say a few words, during which we explained why the church was involved: we told them that we believe everyone is made in the image of God and therefore has inherent dignity and worth, and that human trafficking is arguably the most abhorrent crime that strikes at the heart of this. We told them that we believe in a God of justice, and therefore we want to help them—as men and women employed to bring justice—to be as effective in their jobs as possible. And we told them that in a time when their resources were diminishing but their responsibilities were not, we were well positioned to invest both people power and finances into this area.

At this training session, I again offered more than we knew how to deliver—the leader of my church has joked that I practically offered them a holiday to the Bahamas if they would work with us! This time the police, fire service, our local government, and the housing association asked if we would take the lead in forming a quarterly meeting of the various organisations represented. That is how our church ended up chairing and running the Hastings Anti-Trafficking

Hub (HATH) for three years, during which time we ran training for over four hundred official agency staff, as well as providing further training for 103 of them to equip them to cascade the information throughout their organisations.

Though our local police initially thought that human trafficking wasn't a significant issue in our community, within three years of the inaugural HATH meeting, they had identified over four hundred potential victims and perpetrators of modern slavery in our town and the neighbouring town. They eventually opened a dedicated anti-slavery unit in our local police station, where sixteen partner agencies (including the church) were able to work side by side with the shared aim of seeing perpetrators arrested and brought to justice, victims rescued, and survivors supported and restored. That unit—called the Discovery team—is still operational in Hastings today, and two of the senior officers who have overseen the team have gone on record to state that without the involvement of the local church, this work would never have happened and the dedicated unit would not have come to exist.

God led us on an incredible journey—all started by one church member's vision and relentless pursuit of what Jesus had shown her. We continue to support the police in this area when required, and we can work from the Discovery office whenever we want to. However, now that Discovery is up and running, the church's focus has moved on to reflect the original calling my friend felt God speak to her about: she (along with her team) is now supporting up to a dozen survivors at a time as they seek to rebuild their lives.

I hope this story encourages you on many levels. If you've been living with a vision or passion from God for years, don't be disheartened—keep pursuing him and eventually he will open the doors he's led you to. If you're a church leader or activist who is asked to support local decision makers and authorities in ways that seem unusual, consider going along with the opportunities that arise, seeking to bless those who are responsible for keeping your community safe, and protecting people in your neighbourhood who are vulnerable or oppressed. Channel some of your energy into praying for God to bless your community, and specifically pray for your police, your local government, your fire service, your teachers, and your doctors and judges. Seek innovative ways to support them—the Bible says that Christians have the Holy Spirit and the mind of Christ (1 Cor. 2:16), so we can ask God to give us strategies that others haven't thought of and to show us ways of not only supporting our leaders, but also influencing them.

At the heart of the community

My church is certainly not alone in influencing decision makers in this way and becoming a central player in solutions to community issues. We saw this happen across the country when we went into lockdown due to COVID-19—churches that were well-known in their communities for supporting people in hardship became very involved in local responses to the pandemic.

At Jubilee+ we hear many stories about what churches are doing all across the UK, and often farther afield. For example, when fierce storms hit rural northwest England in December 2015, causing thousands of homes to flood, tens of thousands to be left without power, and an estimated £500 million damage in total, churches were on the front foot.[1] They set up a flood-relief centre, and within a week church volunteers were staffing the centre, clearing out homes, moving rubbish, and doing whatever they could to help. Once the flood waters had started to go down, they opened a café where people affected by the flooding could come for free hot food, and advice from local government and other organisations, and where they could talk about what had happened to them and their homes. Churches in the area also gave out food and cleaning materials. They intentionally worked in partnership across denominations, with other charities and the public sector, throughout the community.

And the work of Cumbrian churches, in partnership with others, didn't end there. They went on to form a response team to plan for future flooding, including running simulated flood alerts, creating a database of people who would need help if it happened again, coordinating teams that could spring into action before flooding hit, and setting up evacuation centres. Working with other local organisations, Christians in the area have gone beyond crisis support to putting in place preventative measures for the good of the whole community.

In a much more urban setting, church leaders such as Ben Lindsay in London have been actively partnering with local politicians, including the Mayor of London, to develop a multi-agency and long-term approach to tackling serious youth violence in the city. Ben's work to engage churches across the nation with the issue of youth violence was mentioned in Parliament by MP Vicky Foxcroft as part of cross-party talks on a long-term strategy to tackle this issue and support young people.[2] Like Ben, some of us are called to influence beyond our locality, having an influence on national policy. That has been the case with Jubilee+ too—we have had opportunities to tell politicians at the highest level about the great work churches are doing in their communities to support people in poverty, but also to use our frontline experience to challenge them to change unfair systems. Most notably, Jubilee+ has been one of a number of charities in the UK speaking out on some of the flaws in the British welfare system, and as a result we have seen a number of changes made to government policy at a national level.

At the same time, we firmly believe that coming to top officials to advocate on behalf of specific individuals is vitally important. This is a key part of speaking up on behalf of those in poverty. Often with poverty comes voicelessness, a lack of opportunity or lack of empowerment to speak up on your own behalf. That is one of the reasons that, for example, the British charity Grace Advocacy[3] was set up. A small number of Christians recognised that people navigating the welfare system had no agency—no power—when sitting in meetings with officials. Unlike consumers, they had nothing to bargain with—they cannot take away their 'business' because they are relying on the system for support. And if they do drop out of the system, often no one cares. With an increasing workload and decreasing resources, it is one less person to help, one less statistic on a form. Advocating to the ones and twos who hold power on behalf of the ones and twos who do not can be just as powerful a testimony to a watching world.

Building relationships with decision makers

All of us can influence at one level or another. Whether you are in a city or a village, whether you are a church leader or member, whether you are advocating on behalf of someone in poverty or sitting in front of the most powerful people in your area, there are a number of ways that we as individual Christians and as church families can meaningfully engage with people who have power in our localities.

First of all—and crucially—we can build relationships with those in our communities who make decisions that affect the poorest and the vulnerable on a local level. I did this when I started working for my local church. With my senior pastor's permission, I arranged meetings with our Member of Parliament, the leader of our local government, my district's chief of police, the head of the local fire department, a top representative of the largest social housing provider in Hastings, elected representatives with relevant responsibilities, and various senior members of staff within our local government, such as the head of community safety.

I went to each of them with the same three questions:

1. What is the biggest problem facing our community, in your opinion?
2. What one issue, if it was completely resolved, would have a disproportionately positive impact on the town?
3. What would you like to see churches such as mine do to help this community?

I jotted down some notes from each meeting, thanked them for their time, and said I would be in touch again soon. Most of them were slightly baffled that I did not meet with them to express an opinion on behalf of the church, but simply to learn from them so that we could make more informed choices about the projects and activities we run. A couple of them were very surprised that I was not asking for money. In fact, one said to me four times in our thirty-minute meeting, 'I haven't got any money to give to the church.' At the end of our time together, when I stood up to leave and he finally realised I really wasn't asking for money, he asked, 'If you set up something on the back of these meetings you're having, how will the church pay for it?' His experience of churches was limited, so he was even more confused when I said, 'Don't worry. We'll pay for it ourselves.'

The purpose of these meetings wasn't to show the decision makers a different side of church life, though it did that in almost every case. It was to get to know our community better through the eyes of those who are working hard on its behalf day in, day out. It was to begin to build relationships with them through which they would see that we are grateful for their service and want to honour their work, encourage them, and join them in making the community we are a part of healthier. We wanted to understand the needs around us so that we wouldn't launch projects just because we wanted to, but because there was a clear role we could play in plugging a gap or supporting what others were doing.

We also made a point of getting to know what other charities in the town were doing, for the same reasons. We didn't want to duplicate something that was already happening. We wanted to bless it and help it to flourish, if we could. For a long time my church (which is a registered charity) has supported another charity in the community as part of our 'local charity of the year' scheme. So when we started to develop a more intentional approach to reflecting God's heart for those facing poverty and injustice, it made sense that the charities we chose were those supporting people in poverty and lifting them out of it. Through the scheme, we raise money for the other charity from September one year to August the next, and especially at our big Christmas and Easter events, and we give it to our nominated charity at the end of the summer. My church owns a conference facility, so we also offer free use of the building if the charity wants to hold an event during the year.

Learning about what is already going on in our communities and coming alongside others—whether statutory agencies or the third sector—to support the often wonderful work they're already doing is a great first step in really demonstrating that a church cares about the town or city where it is.

It is because of the small steps towards engaging with decision makers that we started to take, as a church, from 2011 onwards that when the coronavirus pandemic hit, we were invited to have a seat at the table when a 'community hub' was formed by local government officials. As part of that, we were even asked to chair the Hastings COVID-19 Emergency Food Response Group on behalf of the town. These things don't happen overnight, but the church begins to be seen as having a valid voice when we bless and support others, working with them for the common good of our communities, and especially those in need.

Different churches working together to serve a local area can make an even bigger difference. Projects such as Street Pastors, mentioned earlier in this chapter, are a brilliant example of drawing people from different churches to work together to support the police and other agencies in their work. Often one church will take responsibility for projects such as this but find that the work is more effective—and more sustainable—when they partner with others.

Building relationships with local journalists is important too. The more work we do for the good of those in poverty in our communities, the more likely we are to attract media attention. As a former journalist, I think it's vital for local churches to have someone on their team (paid or voluntary) who knows how to cultivate a healthy relationship with local reporters.

Whether we work with official bodies, other churches, local charities, or journalists, working in partnership is important. Christians and churches do not have a monopoly on good works, and we will be limited in our effectiveness if we do not work with others.

Positive, encouraging, and kind

How we engage with decision makers, charities, and journalists is vitally important. Many of the people in these roles will only hear from community voices when they have a complaint to make. Therefore we have an opportunity to interact with them on a more positive level. That isn't to say we don't complain when something is wrong, but it's better to call for change from a position of general encouragement. When many around us seek to tear people down and bombard them with criticism, we want people with power to know that, yes, we will lobby them to change their opinions and their policies, but at the same time we are 'for' them. We are much more likely to be listened to when we discuss and debate with kindness and openness than when we only want to force the person to change something.

A friend of mine uses the expression, 'We want to leave the other person intact.' So often this thought for the other person's welfare is sadly lacking from public debate, whether that's between politicians or across social media. Christians, however, should be characterised by mercy and compassion. Towards the end of Luke 6, Jesus gives us clear instructions about how to interact with people around us. He includes our enemies; those who hate, curse, or abuse us; those who beg, borrow, or steal from us; those who love us; those who are sinners; even those who are ungrateful and wicked. How we behave to all of these different people actually has nothing whatsoever to do with how they behave towards us. Instead, Jesus sums up what he wants to see in our actions, attitudes, and motivation as this: 'Be merciful, just as your Father is merciful' (Luke 6:36). Indeed, being merciful is one of the things that should distinguish followers of Jesus from those around us.

When we work hard to build positive relationships with decision makers, the media, and other charities, we will find we have many opportunities to show something of the character of God to those around us. We have the chance to behave in a different spirit—often to even 'act in the opposite spirit', as my friend says— empowered by the Holy Spirit.

Positive and proactive engagement with the poorest and the most powerful in our communities makes a huge difference to the way our churches are perceived. Obviously, we don't do it for reputation's sake, but how others think of us is important. Jesus said, 'Let your light shine before others, that they may see your good deeds and glorify your Father in heaven' (Matt. 5:16). Peter, too, writes, 'Live such good lives among the pagans that, though they accuse you of doing wrong, they may see your good deeds and glorify God on the day he visits us' (1 Pet. 2:12).

Even a relatively small thing, such as sending Christmas cards to local decision makers, can make a huge difference. A little note thanking them for their service over the last year, highlighting something specific for which we are grateful, and letting them know our prayers and well wishes are with them can mean a lot.

It can be a series of small acts that result in our, eventually, getting a seat at the table to influence decision makers and bring about change that has a positive impact on those facing poverty and injustice. The voice of the church starts to be heard and valued. One example of this in my own church is that when the news broke that my hometown was ranked thirteenth most deprived community in the country (of 326), we were the second phone call a reporter from one of our local newspapers made. First, he called the Member of Parliament. Second, he called the church. This amazed me at the time. There were so many other people I would have expected him to call before us. In fact, a few years earlier I would have had no expectation that he would call us at all. But because our church is a well-known force for good in the town, he wanted to know what we had to say about Hastings slipping into deeper deprivation than before.

Later that same week, I was also called by a senior police officer in the area to ask if I would be happy to be interviewed by the Home Office[4] on behalf of the church as part of a peer review into how effective Hastings police were at the time when it came to youth and gang crime.

The church *should* have a seat at the table when decisions are being made that affect those in poverty. We have a valuable contribution to make, especially when we are helping people in our communities week by week. People relate to us in a way that they don't always relate to statutory organisations. We should be known as those who have mercy when others run dry and who speak up for those facing injustice even if no one else will. God tells us: 'Seek the welfare of the city where I have sent you into exile, and pray to the LORD on its behalf' and even adds that 'in its welfare you will find your welfare' (Jer. 29:7 ESV).

We cannot seek the welfare of our towns or cities unless we get to know them really well, and that means finding out what others think of them. Not just the powerful, but those in poverty too, and all those in between. If we want to change things for the good of the destitute and those who have no voice, we need to engage positively with powerful people and leaders in the community. This needs to be persistent—not just hit-and-run engagement about the issues we care about, but building for the long-term, cultivating a relationship. We need to offer solutions, not just point out problems. We can expect to hear God speak to us with answers to the issues besetting the 'long devastated places'. And we should expect that as we meaningfully engage with those who have the power to improve the lives of the poorest, we will see change for good.

Study Topics

1. Have you observed that helping people out of a crisis situation is limited in its ability to lift people out of poverty? How do you feel about this?

2. Do you find it easier to help people at their point of need or to speak up on their behalf? Why are both important?

3. If your church closed its doors today, how long do you imagine it would take your community to notice? Who would notice first? Would your answer have been different ten years ago? If so, what has changed?

4. Who are the key decision makers in your area? If you're not already working with them, what could your church do to start engaging with them in a natural and strategic way?

5. How are you actively building relationships with and blessing local government officials, police and fire officers, school teachers, healthcare professionals, charity workers, media representatives, etc.? Are you open to doing things they ask of you, even if you cannot see how it benefits your church? Do you see them as potential partners?

6. Find out about three challenges facing your local government, police force, health facilities, schools, or other public organisations. How might your church help with those challenges? Could you have a part to play in supporting these under-resourced organisations?

CHAPTER SIX

BUYING FOR JUSTICE— THE CREATIVE POWER OF ETHICAL CONSUMERISM

The LORD detests dishonest scales,
> but accurate weights find favour with him.
> (Prov. 11:1)

Whoever oppresses the poor shows contempt for their Maker.
> (Prov. 14:31)

Do not exploit the poor because they are poor,
> and do not crush the needy in court,
for the LORD will take up their case. (Prov. 22:22–23)

Setting the scene—an unjust global economic system

So far we have explored how we can live simple lives, adjusting patterns of behaviour and attitudes to do with how we run our households, handle our money, and treat our possessions. Next we broadened out to look at how we interact with the people around us, and then with the people who make decisions affecting our local area. In many respects it is easier to imagine that our lives can have an impact on poverty when we focus on our individual homes and neighbourhoods, but we can make a difference beyond that—even globally. So we now turn our attention to how we can live poverty-busting lives that have national and international repercussions. The recent coronavirus pandemic has added further urgency to this issue by highlighting the economic vulnerability of so many workers and producers in the developing world.[1]

A few years ago a shopper in a major clothing retailer in the UK was surprised to discover an extra label sewn into a garment. It read: 'Forced to work exhausting hours.' Soon afterwards another garment from the same retailer was found to have a different extra label saying: 'Degrading sweatshop conditions.'[2] It was a cry for help—a cry from the heart. This retailer sources much of its clothing from factories in the developing world where working conditions can often be harsh. For example, exploitation of clothing factory workers in countries like Bangladesh is well-known. Many work in poor conditions for long hours and with very low pay. Yet much of the clothing manufactured in countries like Bangladesh is sold in the West.

In recent times globalisation has linked the economies of the world together as never before. The liberalisation of trading conditions has stimulated international trade. Technology enables easy long-distance transactions. Freight travels faster and more securely than ever before. It can be argued that globalisation should lead to an improved standard of living in developing countries, simply because more trading opportunities should lead to greater demand for their goods and services. Sometimes this happens. However, globalisation more often leads to the reinforcement of the economic power of more developed countries and stronger partners in the marketplace.[3] It is a complex issue. In the midst of this lies the power of the individual consumer—which is the focus of this chapter.

Consumers have power. They create demand. They can also unintentionally support cruel economic exploitation by their purchasing habits. Many consumers never think beyond their own desire for suitable and cheap products. They generally don't ask questions and don't care much about how the things they buy come into the marketplace. However, consumers can choose to resist exploitation when it is identified in a specific supply chain by boycotting particular products or retail companies.

Some consumers in the West have begun to ask more searching questions about the trading policies of the companies from which they purchase key goods like clothing and food. This process has been strengthened by social media and various pressure groups.

In response, major clothing suppliers in countries like the UK have been seeking to demonstrate to their customers that their supply chain is ethical and fair to all the workers in it. My (Martin's) preferred clothing retailer recently stated that it currently sources its garments from 440 factories in twenty-eight countries, linked to a workforce of over half a million.[4] This is a complex supply chain, but you and I can access information about how major retailers manage this process simply by going online.[5]

Why does this matter?

The simple truth is that money equals power. In richer nations, consumers have an ever-increasing amount of disposable income and ever-greater choice in how they spend that money. Internet shopping and a globalised trading environment give us easy access to goods from all parts of the world. However, with spending power there comes responsibility. Our money can serve to exploit and oppress workers elsewhere in the world, even keeping people enslaved, as we'll see below.

Our central concern should be to ensure that buying and selling always provides dignity and an appropriate financial reward for the labour of the provider of goods and services. This does not always happen. Deep injustices exist in trading—often specifically between developed and developing countries. Trading provides a basis for the exploitation of the economically weaker by the economically stronger. Individuals and households have a part to play in this. We all have a responsibility.

This issue should be of particular importance to Christians for a specific reason: the issue of economic justice is a significant theme of the New Testament.

The priority of economic justice in the kingdom of God

It all started in Israel on the banks of the river Jordan with John the Baptist's remarkable prophetic message to the people of his day. He was there to wake up the nation spiritually and prepare them for the coming of Jesus. His preaching was uncompromising and uncomfortable. Significantly, economic justice was high up on his agenda.

John told his listeners that the well-off should not ignore those living in poverty but should share any surplus clothing and food with those in need (Luke 3:11). He told tax collectors not to exploit people by charging them more tax than they really owed (Luke 3:12–13). He told soldiers not to use their power to exploit ordinary citizens by extorting money from them (Luke 3:14). Most of the practical outworking of his message seemed to be about economic justice!

What about Jesus? Didn't he just focus on teaching, healing, and pronouncing forgiveness? Well, not entirely.

Consider a remarkable event in Jesus' ministry. The subject of the story is a man called Zacchaeus who was the senior tax collector in the city of Jericho. He was a Jew who worked for the Roman imperial rulers. The tax system was very open to corruption. The Romans required their tax collectors to give them a set sum of money every year. This money had to be obtained by collecting taxes from the population. However, there was no exact system to decide what each person should pay. The Romans were not too bothered about how the tax collectors resolved the problem, and they turned a blind eye to any tax collectors who collected more than their agreed quota and simply pocketed the surplus!

> Jesus entered Jericho and was passing through. A man was there by the name of Zacchaeus; he was a chief tax collector and was wealthy. He wanted to see who Jesus was, but because he was short he could not see over the crowd. So he ran ahead and climbed a sycamore-fig tree to see him, since Jesus was coming that way.

When Jesus reached the spot, he looked up and said to him, 'Zacchaeus, come down immediately. I must stay at your house today.' So he came down at once and welcomed him gladly.

All the people saw this and began to mutter, 'He has gone to be the guest of a sinner.'

But Zacchaeus stood up and said to the Lord, 'Look, Lord! Here and now I give half of my possessions to the poor, and if I have cheated anybody out of anything, I will pay back four times the amount.'

Jesus said to him, 'Today salvation has come to this house, because this man, too, is a son of Abraham. For the Son of Man came to seek and to save the lost.' (Luke 19:1–10)

Zacchaeus had clearly been using the taxation system to make a lot of money for himself—and in doing so, he had exploited ordinary citizens of Jericho by charging them over the odds for their tax payments. After spending time in the presence of Jesus, however, he openly acknowledged that he had 'cheated' people out of their money and he wanted to make restitution.

As we see elsewhere in the Gospels, Jesus put economic justice at the heart of discipleship. When we draw close to Jesus, we begin to catch his heart, and it affects what we do with our money.

Now consider an important incident from the last week of Jesus' life when he was spending time in the temple compound in Jerusalem. He was teaching and healing and drawing significant crowds. On one occasion he took everyone completely by surprise:

> On reaching Jerusalem, Jesus entered the temple courts and began driving out those who were buying and selling there. He overturned the tables of the money-changers and the benches of those selling doves, and would not allow anyone to carry merchandise through the temple courts. And as he taught them, he said, 'Is it not written: "My house will be called a house of prayer for all nations"? But you have made it "a den of robbers".' (Mark 11:15–17)

Jesus totally disrupted the trading market in the temple compound. This market was run by the priests and was supposed to help ordinary Jewish pilgrims who came to the temple to make sacrifices and perform their religious duties. Many people needed to buy animals to make the required sacrifices. Also, there was a rule that the standard coinage provided by the Roman rulers could not be used for any transactions in the temple compound. As a result, people had to exchange their Roman coins for specially minted temple coinage in order to buy anything from the market. This might all seem reasonable enough until we realise that the temple market was a monopoly controlled by the priests. Prices could easily be heavily inflated—and they were! Exchange rates were fixed to be favourable to the money-changers. Any monopoly produces the exploitation of those who depend on its goods and services. Thousands of Jewish pilgrims depended on the temple market—and were heavily exploited through monopoly trading. This made Jesus very angry and he challenged it head-on!

Economic justice mattered to Jesus.

What about the apostles? Did they have anything to say about economic justice? Yes they did! Consider this powerful statement from James, the half brother of Jesus, who for many years led the Jerusalem church and was a highly respected leader:

> Now listen, you rich people, weep and wail because of the misery that is coming on you. Your wealth has rotted, and moths have eaten your clothes. Your gold and silver are corroded. Their corrosion will testify against you and eat your flesh like fire. You have hoarded wealth in the last days. Look! The wages you failed to pay the workers who mowed your fields are crying out against you. The cries of the harvesters have reached the ears of the Lord Almighty. You have lived on earth in luxury and self-indulgence. You have fattened yourselves in the day of slaughter. You have condemned and murdered the innocent one, who was not opposing you. (James 5:1–6)

What is the context of this remarkable outburst? James was writing a circular letter to Jewish Christians who had been dispersed from their homes in Judea by persecution. With very few resources they were now seeking to settle in foreign countries in the eastern Roman Empire. James appears to have heard that some of these believers had been heavily exploited when working as day labourers on farms. In those days, a labourer's wage was usually paid at the end of every working day. James proclaims forthcoming divine judgement on those who did not pay proper wages to their workers but pocketed the money for themselves.

The apostles were passionate about economic justice and willing to speak up on behalf of those being exploited.

Economic justice—then and now

How does all this relate to our lives in the modern developed world as we seek to work out how to be disciples of Christ? Where does economic justice fit in to our personal lives? These questions seem particularly hard to address because in modern life we usually have very little direct contact with the producers of the goods we buy. These faceless people are invisible to us as we stroll down the aisles of our attractive high street shops or as we scroll through the pages of our well-presented online stores. It is only in poorer countries, where market trading or bartering remains important, that consumers can regularly see and talk to the people who produce the goods and services they buy.

Let's think about this for a moment. Generally speaking, we have become very detached from the people we buy things from. We don't know them or meet them. We don't know much about their lives. This detachment can have negative and unintended consequences. It can mean we don't care about the way they live—and the possible economic injustice which may lie behind some of the things we can so easily buy. This reality is fairly obvious when we buy things made in other countries. However, have you ever given much thought to the drivers who travel relentlessly to deliver packages from online retailers to your home? Or the workers who are often hidden away in vast warehouses working under tremendous time pressure to ensure that your order reaches your home at breakneck speed?[6]

And what about the pay gap? In the UK, there are still big differences in pay for men and women doing the same jobs,[7] and ethnic minorities are frequently paid less than their white colleagues too.[8] The UK obviously isn't alone in this. These types of pay gaps are seen throughout the world.

Consider 'zero-hour contracts'. In the UK it is currently legal to use employment contracts with no fixed working hours.[9] This is convenient and suitable for some workers, but for the majority it provides the basis for serious exploitation in terms of rates of pay, conditions of work, and huge uncertainty of working hours and income levels.[10] Similar flexible contracts are used in many countries but can be frequently abused by employers.

So how do we start addressing these issues as consumers? A good place to begin is to consider three very different but important modern Christian initiatives which have, in a variety of ways, addressed the economic justice priorities of Christian discipleship. We will look briefly at each of these and seek to find relevant applications in terms of our personal lifestyles and economic decision-making. Then, in conclusion, we will look more widely at how Christians can engage with other secular initiatives which focus on ethical consumer purchasing.

Christians and economic justice— pioneers of the fair trade movement

While the problems noted above persist, in recent decades there have been pockets of change in the West around the ethics of consumer purchasing. In the UK this really got started in the 1970s—and Christians were at the forefront of the change. In 1970, the Christian sociologist Richard Adams made his first visit to India.[11] In a research project he discovered that farmers were getting very small amounts of money for their produce and that various middlemen were taking the major share of the profits when agricultural products went to market or were sold internationally. Adams realised that however hard these farmers worked they could not escape severe poverty. They were trapped in their current trading environment. He also noticed that the same economic stranglehold was operating for craft and clothing producers. From this experience, Adams decided to try to create trading organisations in the UK which could import goods from the developing world in such a way that the original producers received a meaningful and appropriate wage which would help lift them out of poverty. This was a ground-breaking idea. Within a few years Adams pioneered 'Tearcraft', which was, for a time, the trading arm of the Christian relief charity Tearfund. Then, in 1979, he went on to found 'Traidcraft', a company solely committed to creating a new type of economic relationship between producers and consumers. Adams describes his vision: 'The original concept behind Traidcraft was to set up a business in which those living in poverty in developing countries would get a better price for their produce or work than they could through conventional business. It was to introduce equity into the trading process.'[12] Traidcraft's slogan became 'Fighting poverty through trade'. It positioned itself as a business based on the application of Christian principles. Its initial and primary marketplace was in churches—through stalls, coffee mornings, and special events. The churches proved to be a very vigorous and widespread support base. Many churches from differing traditions embraced the opportunity to provide a place for Traidcraft to sell its goods. In this way, during the 1980s, churches became the first significant marketplace in the UK for fair trade goods. The support of the churches enabled Traidcraft to grow and diversify its business. In this way its influence spread. Others saw Traidcraft's business model and started to replicate it.

Traidcraft's story is full of firsts.[13] Between 1981 and 1985 it pioneered the first fair trade tea, coffee, sugar, and chocolate brought into the UK. This was followed by the introduction of the first significant fair trade clothing ranges in 1987. Then in 1991, Traidcraft helped to found the coffee brand 'Cafédirect', which was the first fair trade product ever to reach the supermarket shelves. A few years later, in 1999, Traidcraft introduced the 'GEOBAR', a cereal bar which was the first UK-made product made using several fairly traded imported ingredients.

However, Traidcraft's main importance lies in its influence on the wider trading environment. 'Traidcraft Exchange' was established in 1986 to promote the principles and practice of fair trade more widely. Then a key event took place in 1992 when Traidcraft co-founded the 'Fairtrade Foundation' which now licenses the use of the 'Fairtrade' mark for products on sale in the UK.[14] Interestingly, two of the other five co-founders, Christian Aid and CAFOD, were also motivated specifically by Christian values.[15]

The establishment of the Fairtrade Foundation started to bring fair trade into the commercial mainstream in the UK and led to major retailers marketing more and more fair trade products as well as developing fair trade ranges of their own. The Fairtrade Foundation established rigorous criteria for identifying fair trade. These included appropriate remuneration for the producers and the investment of a fair trade 'premium' in the improvement of living and working conditions among producers. There are now, at the time of this writing, over six thousand registered fair trade products on sale in the UK.[16] The 'Fairtrade mark' is now well recognised by consumers. Fair trade has become a significant part of the business and retailing culture of the UK.

The growth of fair trade in the UK is paralleled by developments in Europe, in North America, and in many developing countries. The UK Fairtrade Foundation is now working in strategic partnerships with similar organisations across the world.[17]

The fair trade movement is principally an ethically driven movement. It has played its part in the development of the growing 'trade justice' movement which addresses the important structural issues of the terms of international trade.[18] Trade justice is a vital issue, but our focus in this chapter is on individual discipleship and its implications for us as consumers. Fair trade buying habits and priorities are an important contemporary application of the place of economic justice in Christian discipleship. This can be enhanced by churches which use fairly traded goods. Such churches can join the 'Fairtrade Churches' scheme in the UK which currently has over 7,500 member churches.[19]

Christians and economic justice—on the frontline in the fight against modern slavery

Just before I wrote this chapter a major news story hit the headlines in the UK.[20] Police had uncovered the largest modern slavery network ever discovered in the country. A Polish criminal gang, based in the UK, had persuaded several hundred fellow Poles to move to the UK with the promise of a better life. However, on arrival, the victims had their identity papers taken away. They were forced to live in inhumane conditions, kept together and under constant guard. Then they were made to do menial work in recycling centres and farms while their minders confiscated their wages. Gang members lived in luxury whilst their victims suffered poverty, ill health, isolation, and regular threats of punishment if they sought to escape.

Significantly, it was the outreach workers of a Christian anti-trafficking charity who first identified the victims.[21] They helped them, gained their trust, and then provided key information to the police which ultimately led to the trial, conviction, and imprisonment of the key gang members.

Modern slavery has many facets. However, there are three main types of slavery in operation round the world. Firstly, enslavement of adults based on forced labour, as in the case discussed above. Secondly, slavery focusing on the exploitation of women and girls who are forcibly controlled or trafficked as sex slaves. Thirdly, slavery which harshly oppresses children by luring or coercing them into child labour.[22]

Modern slavery is everywhere—as we saw in chapter four. It is a worldwide problem and no country is immune. Modern slavery crosses continents as well as takes place within national boundaries. Modern slavery in one form or another will almost certainly be operating near where you live. For example, you may have unwittingly supported modern slavery through using a car wash. If a car wash is too cheap, then the people working there are not likely to be paid very much—if anything at all.[23] A recent conversation I had with the police officer responsible for modern slavery issues in my rural area of England brought home to me the reality that sex trafficking in my town and the forced labour of migrant workers on nearby farms is a real but totally unseen issue right on my doorstep. Natalie, too, in her seaside town 250 miles from my area, found through working with her local police that there was a property housing eleven slaves in her own street! It has been estimated that there are currently about forty million people worldwide in forced labour, sexual exploitation, and domestic servitude.[24] Indeed, there are more people enslaved today than were transported in the entire period of the European-led transatlantic slave trade.[25]

In recent years Christians have been very active in the fight against modern slavery in two main ways.

Firstly, Christians have been prominent in seeking to influence public policy. For example, in the UK, the formulation of the Modern Slavery Act (2015) received significant input from a variety of Christian activists and pressure groups. The Act strengthened the criminal justice process and created a new independent Anti-Slavery Commissioner to oversee the issue on behalf of the Government.

Secondly, key Christian organisations are at the forefront of raising awareness, investigating possible slavery networks, giving key support to victims, providing legal advocacy, and supporting law enforcement.[26] I have had the privilege of working with several of these organisations in the UK. It is important for Christians to get behind such organisations in support, finance, and prayer.

However, for our purposes, we need to focus on another aspect of this issue. Our theme is economic justice—and in particular we are considering the responsibility of Christians in their personal economic decision-making as consumers.

The battle against slavery needs to be fought through consumer pressure as well as through specialist agencies and public policy. William Wilberforce and the campaigners against the eighteenth-century transatlantic slave trade understood the importance of consumer pressure.[27] In their situation it was easy to identify the consumer products which were based on slave labour. Sugar from the Caribbean was the obvious one—as it was produced on plantations using slave labour. So the abolitionists organised a consumer boycott of sugar. It is estimated that about 300,000 people joined the boycott, and this had a significant impact on the market for sugar in the UK, thus undermining the economic benefits of using slavery. The sugar boycott greatly helped the abolitionist campaign and served to expose the workings of the slave trade more clearly. Despite the advantages of social media platforms for mass publicity, boycotts such as this are perhaps harder to mobilise in today's consumerist society, in which we are often strongly attached to the products under scrutiny and can be prone to prioritising our own preferences above the concerns of justice.

Modern slavery is more complex. It is mostly hidden and it is multifaceted. However, consumer pressure is still an important aspect of the current campaign to rid the world of modern slavery. The things we buy in developed countries could easily have economic slavery in the supply chain, especially if goods are imported from the developing world. The Modern Slavery Act in the UK has required large companies to review their trading policies and report on any issues with modern slavery in their supply chains. These reports are generally available online. As Christian consumers we can be influential by taking an active interest in this information from the large companies we regularly buy from. For example, not only do I often push a trolley around the aisles of my favoured local supermarket, but I also keep up-to-date with published information from this company on its supply chain. You can do the same with the large retailers you commonly buy from. It is generally fairly simple to go online and look for their updates.[28] Alternatively, you can email their customer relations team and ask for information from them. The more people there are who do this, the more our major retailers will keep alert on this issue. This, in turn, will cause retailers to remain vigilant in their supply chains.

Remember, consumers have power.

There is another important aspect to this issue. Christians who have influence in their workplace or who run businesses have an important role to play. Many of our workplaces and companies may also be at risk of accidentally involving modern slavery in their supply chain. However, they can receive expert advice and support by joining organisations such as the Slave-free Alliance, which provides expert business advice in this area.[29] A simple action like this is a demonstration of awareness and concern and will strengthen the fight against modern slavery in the supply chain.

Christians and economic justice— developing the foodbank movement

One of the major church-based social action initiatives in the UK in recent years has been the foodbank movement. Since the financial crisis of 2008, and the subsequent changes in the welfare system, there has been a vast growth in the number of church-based foodbanks in the UK. There are now over 1,200 outlets across the country[30] and hundreds of thousands of people have been the beneficiaries of emergency food supplies. Foodbanks have become a frontline of practical concern for economic justice among the churches. They support large numbers of people who have fallen prey to personal debt, been penalised by benefits reforms, or struggled to find work.

Our concern here is to identify the practical economic justice implications of the foodbank movement for Christians. There are three different implications to consider.

Firstly, the foodbank movement has led large numbers of Christians to start giving significant quantities of food away in the form of donations to foodbanks (or a cash equivalent). Many people now have this in mind when they do their food shopping— buying specific products with the aim of immediately giving them away. Significantly, this is very reminiscent of the response John the Baptist demanded from affluent people in his day: 'Anyone who has two shirts should share with the one who has none, and anyone who has food should do the same' (Luke 3:11). Have you ever thought of checking to see if your favoured food supermarket supports local foodbanks? If so, thank them for doing so and tell them that this is a factor in your decision to keep shopping there. If not, challenge them to do so. If they are unwilling to support local foodbanks, why not be radical and change supermarkets? Remember, consumers have power.

Secondly, many Christians have given up their free time to volunteer at foodbanks. This is also significant. More and more Christians (alongside many others) are willing to give their time and energy to help those experiencing food poverty. However, we need to do more than simply a bit of volunteering. Thinking about the lives of the clients we encounter at foodbanks is important. We need to let our hearts be touched by God's mercy towards them, and go beyond helping at arm's length to actually sharing our own meals with others, becoming friends with them.

Thirdly, another implication of food poverty has recently come into focus—food waste. The extraordinarily high level of food waste in the UK food supply chain has become much better known. In recent years some of this waste food has been given to foodbanks, soup kitchens, or other charities rather than being consigned to the bin. This is an economic justice issue. We cannot be at ease in a society in which so much food is wasted while many thousands of people experience food poverty. However, food waste is not only a commercial problem—huge amounts of food are also thrown away in many households! This fact brings the reality closer to home, literally.

Let's consider some statistics on UK food waste. Recent research tells us the shocking reality: over three million metric tonnes of food are wasted annually in the food supply chain, and on top of this there are over seven million tonnes of household food waste every year![31] There are just over twenty-seven million households in the UK.[32] If we divide seven million tonnes of food waste between twenty-seven million households, that makes an average level of food waste per household every year a little over a quarter of a tonne (about 250 kilograms or 550 pounds). These numbers should cause us to pause whenever we are buying food and ask ourselves whether we really need the quantity and variety we are purchasing.

Food has become a barometer of the social conscience of the nation. Food is an economic justice issue. Food is a frontline issue for consumers. Therefore, Christian discipleship should lead us, as consumers, to facilitate the redistribution of surplus food to overcome food poverty and to be at the forefront of efforts to avoid food waste.

Engaging with the wider ethical consumer culture

Christians have no monopoly in the concern for economic justice through consumer habits. In the UK, numerous small companies as well as a few major retailers represent this concern.[33] It is good to look out for businesses that are committed to fair trade principles and focused on the quest for economic justice in retailing and consumer habits in the developed world.[34]

Some final reflections

We are all consumers. We are all buying a large variety of products all the time. Unthinking consumerism is the enemy of Christian discipleship. It's not enough to donate some tins of food to a foodbank or some of your time to a night shelter. If we want to take steps towards living out a poverty-busting lifestyle, then we need to examine our patterns of consumer purchasing. There are often more options than we realise.

Consumers have power. Let's use that power in the fight for economic justice.

Study Topics

Let's take time to reflect on the practical implications of this chapter for us as individuals, families, households, and churches. Remember, our focus has been on our lifestyles. We are seeking to find ways to move towards a poverty-busting lifestyle in which our ordinary consumer habits reflect our wider concern and engagement in practical efforts to overcome poverty in our communities and in the wider world.

1. Read through the story of Zacchaeus in Luke 19:1–10. Why is this story so significant for our understanding of the economic justice dimension of Christian discipleship? What effect would Zacchaeus' change of lifestyle have had on him and on his family?

2. To what extent are you engaging with and using fair trade products? How has this chapter helped you understand the wider importance of fair trade? Do you plan to make any changes to your lifestyle? If so, how will you implement these changes? What three changes could you make to your weekly shop?

3. To what extent are you involved in foodbanks? What is the most important thing about the discussion of food-banks in this chapter? Is there any practical outworking you have in mind for yourself/your household?

4. What have you learnt about modern slavery in this chapter? Can you see any practical ways you can respond to this challenge?

5. In what ways could your church engage more strategically in the battle for economic justice?

CHAPTER SEVEN

CARE FOR CREATION – AND ITS IMPLICATIONS FOR SOCIAL JUSTICE

Where it all began ...

This part of my (Martin's) personal story started fifteen years ago. My wife and I decided to sit down one day and thoroughly review our lifestyle. We wanted to follow the discipleship ethos of 'simplicity', which I discussed in chapter 3. We also had in mind our growing concern for the environment, so we took a close look at the ways in which our family could be more environmentally friendly. We did a lot of talking and thinking. Then we moved quickly to turn ideas into action.

Our starting point was that we wanted to live, to the best of our ability, with a strong focus on care for creation. We made a wide range of new lifestyle choices as a result. We installed various energy-saving devices in our home. Then, a little later on, when we had the money to do so, we installed solar panels. We consciously chose to use public transport when possible. We chose to run an economic car. We avoided becoming a two-car family by the use of a 50cc motor scooter and bicycles. We decided to source our electricity from a different supplier which was committed to investing a high proportion of its profits into the development of renewable energy. We switched our bank to one more committed to environmental policies and investments. We focused on recycling. We tried to reduce food waste. We started to actively consider environmental issues in our purchasing practices. We adopted water-saving strategies.

These were all very conscious choices—and we have stuck to them over the past fifteen years. We have also made other changes along the way. For example, I need to fly quite often, mostly with work commitments. Flying causes pollution and is very carbon-intensive, having a direct impact on climate change. However, when we need to fly we can take action to protect the environment. I have adopted a way of doing this. It is called 'carbon offsetting' and involves putting money into such things as tree planting.[1]

So why did we do these things? Looking back I think there were three main reasons. Firstly, we were becoming increasingly aware of environmental issues through the media and public discussion. Secondly, we were trying not to be wasteful simply because we were concerned about the sheer amount of waste our consumer society was producing. Thirdly, and most importantly, we were more and more convinced about the biblical case for the care of creation as a part of Christian discipleship.

Let's look at this last point more closely before we move on. Obviously, the Bible cannot tell us directly about modern environmental issues because such issues did not exist in the same way in biblical times. The Bible can, though, give us perspectives through which to interpret the current challenges. So let's begin with the Old Testament. Genesis is the key text for us in this matter. There are three fundamental truths which Genesis teaches about creation which are essential to understand and embrace.

Genesis truths No. 1: God created it all!

The opening words of Genesis say it loud and clear—God created the world and it ultimately belongs to him: 'In the beginning God created the heavens and the earth. Now the earth was formless and empty, darkness was over the face of the deep, and the Spirit of God was hovering over the waters. And God said, "Let there be light," and there was light' (Gen. 1:1–3).

The world is a designed reality and it has a purpose. It did not come about by chance. Nor did the wonderful array of life which fills the earth come about by natural processes alone. It was designed—and then blessed by God in its development and emerging diversity. This is a very counter-cultural statement in the modern Western world in which secular thinking has increasingly proposed the idea that life is self-generating or self-explanatory. The Bible contradicts this assertion firmly—consistently affirming that God is the creator and the sustainer of all life (e.g., Ps. 104; John 1:1–3; Col. 1:17; Heb. 1:1–3).

Modern, city-dwelling, Westernised people have largely lost touch with the natural world. Many of us live in a world in which the natural world is peripheral to our experience. Yes, we have parks and trees and small gardens, but many of us have little contact with farming, with the wild places, with the hills and mountains, and with the wildlife which exists all around us. We need to recapture something of the experience of engaging with the natural world on its own terms and learning again that it reflects something of God's glory—that it points to its creator and points us to our creator too!

Genesis truths No. 2: We are God's 'stewards' of the earth

In the first mention of mankind in the creation account, we discover that we were created specifically to develop, cultivate, and protect the world:

> Then God said, 'Let us make mankind in our image, in our likeness, so that they may rule over the fish in the sea and the birds in the sky, over the livestock and all the wild animals, and over all the creatures that move along the ground.'

> So God created mankind in his own image,
>   in the image of God he created them;
>   male and female he created them.

> God blessed them and said to them, 'Be fruitful and increase in number; fill the earth and subdue it. Rule over the fish of the sea and the

birds of the sky and over every living creature that
moves on the ground.' (Gen. 1:26–28)

This is an insight of the utmost importance which shapes our
whole outlook. Humanity has a mandate and responsibility from God
which is rightly understood as 'stewardship'. We are commanded to
look after creation on behalf of God as his delegated representatives.
This means that we are not free to exploit and degrade the earth and its
resources, which would mean going against God's purposes. Modern
consumerism makes us think that the environment is just something
to be used for our benefit. A biblical perspective tells a different
story—we are gardeners in his garden, we are farmers on his land, we
are tenants in his house. The created world belongs to God, not to us.[2]

Genesis truths No. 3: the power of sin has deeply affected the environment

Thirdly, Genesis 3 vividly describes mankind's fall into sin. We should
not underestimate the importance of this tragic event in explaining
the world around us. The 'fall of man' is about broken relationships
and disrupted harmony within the creation. First and foremost,
Adam and Eve were separated from their original close relationship
with God—and symbolically they were forced out of the Garden of
Eden (Gen. 3:23–24). After this we see tension and difficulty arising
in human relationships as a result of the selfishness arising from sin.
However, for our purposes, there is another dimension of the fall of
man which needs consideration. After the fall of man there came
some new and harsh realities: disruption, difficulty, and dysfunction

in the relationship between mankind and the created world. This is initially described in the poetic language of God's curse in Genesis 3:

> Cursed is the ground because of you;
>> through painful toil you will eat food from it
>> all the days of your life.
> It will produce thorns and thistles for you,
>> and you will eat the plants of the field.
> By the sweat of your brow
>> you will eat your food
> until you return to the ground,
>> since from it you were taken;
> for dust you are
>> and to dust you will return. (vv. 17–19)

This is a prophetic prediction of a new and complex relationship between mankind and the natural world. After the fall of man the earth would no longer be so utterly productive and easy to manage as in the original creation. There would be difficulties managing the earth's resources and a partial decline in its capacities. This insight helps to explain the tension we experience between the incredible fertility and abundance of the natural world on the one hand and, on the other, its vulnerability to disease, destructive weather conditions, natural disasters, and the negative influences of human exploitation.

Let's take a look at this issue from a New Testament perspective, where we are confronted with the coming of the kingdom of God through Jesus (Mark 1:14–15). As a result, salvation through the gospel of Jesus Christ is the central reality (Rom. 1:16; 3:21–26). Salvation appears to start at the level of the individual. We can each find personal salvation through faith in Christ. Then we notice the importance of the church—the living community of faith (1 Cor. 12:12–27; Eph. 2:19–22). Believers are intended for community. And it isn't long before we also realise that when Christ returns he will dramatically renew creation and bring about a 'new heaven and a new earth' (Rev. 19–22). The community of believers is going to be redeemed alongside the whole of creation! However, in the meantime, despite the arrival of the kingdom of God, Paul gives a very vivid account of the current impact of sin on the created order in his moving and profound description of the unresolved problems of the world under the power of sin:

> I consider that our present sufferings are not worth comparing with the glory that will be revealed in us. For the creation waits in eager expectation for the children of God to be revealed. For the creation was subjected to frustration, not by its own choice, but by the will of the one who subjected it, in hope that the creation itself will be liberated from its bondage to decay and brought into the freedom and glory of the children of God. (Rom. 8:18–21)

Here Paul makes clear that the natural world was directly impacted by mankind's 'fall' into rebellion against God. As a result, the natural world is currently unable to fulfil its potential and will, to some extent, malfunction. This will only be overcome at the end-time second coming of Jesus when 'the children of God' will be 'revealed'. This event will enable the creation to be 'liberated from its bondage to decay and brought into the freedom and glory of the children of God'. This is a vital biblical perspective which helps us, as disciples, to think and act decisively in our care of creation.

So what are the implications of all this for Christians? We have to go back to the beginning—to Genesis. We are 'stewards'. The environment is our responsibility. God gave it to us to look after. Both our stewardship of it and its response to any care we do give it have gone badly wrong due to the power of sin. However, Christians should be at the forefront in any society in caring for creation and considering the protection of the environment. It should be a part of our day-to-day discipleship. It is our prophetic responsibility to be 'stewards' of creation.

Having briefly and simply set out this biblical framework, we can now turn to look at some of the most important environmental issues we face.

Pollution—the degradation of the environment

Pollution comes in many forms. In recent years it has become a central environmental issue with global implications.

I visited Romania in 1990 shortly after the fall of the Communist regime. I stayed in a coal-mining area only to discover that they washed the coal in the main river—thereby causing the water to change colour dramatically and creating very polluted water for everyone living downstream. There were massive environmental and health implications. It was distressing to see.

Water pollution, such as I experienced in Romania, is a major problem, especially in the developing world, leading to serious risks to human health and to food production. Every day about six thousand children die of water-related diseases.[3] Right now about 785 million people do not have clean water available close to their homes.[4]

Some years ago I visited Cairo, the sprawling capital city of Egypt, which is renowned for its heavily overcrowded roads. On my first day there I went for a short jog around the streets in the early evening, only to find that my breathing was so affected by the massive air pollution caused by road vehicles that I was hardly able to run due to tightening in my chest. It was a shocking experience—but it was even more distressing to think of the implications for local people.

Air pollution, such as I experienced in Cairo, is a major and growing problem in urban environments throughout the world, leading to many significant health problems. According to the World Health Organisation, air pollution causes the deaths of about eight million people every year across the world.[5]

I visited Nairobi in Kenya a few years ago. I spent time in various parts of the city and visited its main slum area, Kibera—one of Africa's largest slums. Rubbish was evident throughout the city—but there were mountains of rubbish in and around Kibera. Rubbish on the streets, rubbish in the walkways, rubbish in the open spaces, rubbish in the streams. Scenes like this can be experienced all over the developing world. Most people in the Western world have never considered what they would do if their rubbish was not collected regularly. It is worth thinking about.

Rubbish pollution, such as I experienced in Nairobi, is a major health hazard in many parts of the world. A quarter of the world's population does not have its rubbish collected.[6] The poorer the country the more likely that rubbish pollution adversely affects its citizens, especially in urban environments.

A short while ago my wife and I went on holiday to a coastal area in Wales, in the UK. We stayed right by the sea. I cycled long distances along the coastal cycle path. Everywhere there was evidence of plastic on the beach and in the sea—especially plastic bottles. It never used to be this way when I visited this coastal area fifty years ago as a child. Something has changed. Almost anywhere in the world people are noticing the ever-growing amounts of plastic items in waterways and in the sea (and among the other general rubbish around us).[7] In 2018 Greenpeace calculated that '16 million plastic bottles in the UK end up in our environment' every day.[8] In richer countries there has been a significant investment in plastic collection and recycling. Poorer nations simply do not have the financial resources to do the same.

Plastic pollution is a growing environmental challenge. Huge quantities of plastic have ended up in the seas of the world, causing serious dangers for fish and threatening to degrade the oceans as the plastic gradually breaks down over long periods of time. Even when it has decomposed it remains a serious environmental threat in the form of micro-plastics which poison marine life and can easily enter the food chain. Recent research tells us that globally only about 9 percent of plastic is recycled, whilst about 12 percent is incinerated and about 79 percent stays around.[9]

Pollution is a vital environmental issue. It comes in many forms and manifests itself in different ways in different places. It is a real threat to the well-being of humanity in the coming decades as the world's population continues to rise and as different forms of pollution pose significant health risks and undermine food production for many millions of people, especially in developing countries. It needs to be taken seriously by Christians and churches.

The urgent issue for today—climate change

About twelve years ago I was invited to a special meeting in my town. I was told there was going to be an important scientist coming to speak on climate change. I knew a little about climate change and was aware that it was an important and controversial issue. I was intrigued, so I went to the meeting. The speaker turned out to be one of the world's leading climate scientists, Professor John Houghton, who had recently retired from working with the UN helping to head up their worldwide climate change research. Prof Houghton spoke eloquently and made an impassioned plea for Christians to be involved in environmentalism. I had the opportunity to speak to him at the end. It was one of the most important conversations I have ever had.

I left that meeting convinced for the first time about the foundational importance of climate change and certain that this was a top priority for Christians. I researched the issue carefully and came to understand some of its key features. I learnt more about the rise in surface temperatures, the melting of the ice caps, and the negative impact of deforestation and rising sea levels. I understood that almost all climate change has been created by human actions—specifically the burning of fossil fuels. However, I was struck by the fact that our experience of the impact of climate change in countries like the UK is currently relatively mild. Severe flooding is on the increase but is generally managed by public agencies, although we should not underestimate the impact on those affected, who are often lower earners who can only afford housing on flood plains. Warmer summers are still generally appreciated, despite the rising risks to farming yields caused by water shortages. The effects of occasional severe short droughts can be partially reduced by an integrated water management system across the whole nation. In the UK we are currently largely insulated from the worst effects of climate change. This may change in the coming years, but right now it is in stark contrast to the experience of those living in many developing nations.

Climate change—voices from the developing world

Recently I was on a visit to Zambia. I have various involvements there, including representing a church-based charity which is sponsoring a significant farming project for smallholders.[10] My flight had a stopover in Harare in Zimbabwe. A friendly and conversational black Zimbabwean man came on board and sat next to me for the final leg of my journey to Lusaka, the capital of Zambia. We got talking. He quickly told me his story. He had left Zimbabwe for the USA about twenty years ago due to the political oppression of the Mugabe regime. His wider family stayed in Zimbabwe, and they own land—but this land has been much less productive in recent years. 'Why is this?' I asked, thinking his answer would be mainly about the problems caused by the oppressive and corrupt political regime. 'The main reason,' he answered, without hesitation, 'is climate change.' Then he got animated and turned and looked straight at me. 'When I was growing up, the rainfall was predictable and sufficient. With good irrigation our land was very productive—Zimbabwe was known then as "the breadbasket of Africa". But now, there is much less rain, people don't know when to expect it, and there is a constant risk of drought. Harvests have been declining for years—and it is the poor who pay the heaviest price.'

This is not the first time I have heard this type of story. During the past decade I've travelled to quite a few places in Africa and Asia due to my work. I always seek opportunities to ask people about rainfall levels, climate change, and agriculture—and I invariably get the same type of answer. Climate change is a well-recognised reality in tropical and developing countries. There is widespread anxiety about the risks to agriculture and food production caused by global warming leading to a more unpredictable and extreme climate. Extreme flooding and extended droughts are both becoming more common. Rainfall patterns are noticeably less predictable. All these factors have major impacts on all forms of agriculture.

The science of climate change and global warming

So what is going on? The study of the climate is one of the biggest international scientific enterprises ever undertaken. Much of it is sponsored by the UN. It involves scientific collaboration on an enormous scale across the world. In 1988 the UN set up the Intergovernmental Panel on Climate Change (IPCC) to facilitate this research and to provide authoritative briefings.[11] I've had the privilege over recent years to be invited as a 'faith community' representative to IPCC briefings in the UK. The work of the IPCC has demonstrated beyond reasonable doubt that the climate is changing significantly and that the average temperatures on the earth are rising steadily. What is the primary reason for this? Simply stated, most climate change is caused by human economic activity—especially the production of vast amounts of carbon dioxide and other so-called greenhouse gases through the burning of fossil fuels and other industrial processes.[12] An initially sceptical Western general public is now coming to realise that this is a reality and that it matters. There is a growing sense of urgency emerging—especially among young people.

Climate change is a vast and complex process with various significant and concerning outcomes.[13] In this section I want to focus on one key impact of climate change and look at its significance for living a poverty-busting lifestyle.[14]

Scientists tell us that a central outcome of the global warming produced by climate change is, in their words, 'the intensification of the hydrological cycle'.[15] So what does that mean? In simple terms, it means that everything to do with rainfall will become more extreme due to global warming. The basic reason for this is that, as surface and air temperatures increase due to global warming, more water evaporates into the air. Warmer air can hold more water vapour, which often leads to more intense rainfall. But while some areas experience more intense rainfall, others experience more droughts. This is because if the increased evaporation of water into the air is not followed by rainfall, due to other factors in the weather system such as wind patterns, then the soil in those areas becomes dryer and dryer. Therefore, on the one hand, there will be higher instances of heavy rainfall, flooding, and storms, whilst, on the other hand, there will be more periods of unusually low rainfall and drought. They are two sides of the same coin—and that coin is 'the intensification of the hydrological cycle'.

But what is the significance of all this for our purposes? This pattern of more intense rainfall and greater water shortage is more extreme in countries with hotter climates—and the poorest developing countries are largely in hotter, tropical or semi-tropical parts of the world. In temperate climates, such as in most of Europe, these variations are usually moderate and can currently be managed by technology such as flood defences or complex water management systems. The implication of this is that nations in areas such as Europe and North America can ride out the extremes fairly well. The same is not true in hotter climates where the intense rainfall is harder to control, often leads to extensive damage from flooding, and where chronic water shortage, drought, and unpredictable rainfall are causing ever-increasing difficulties in food production.

Caring for creation—and caring for those in poverty

This leads us to a challenging conclusion—global warming caused by climate change is a direct social justice issue. Or, to put it another way, the things we do in richer, developed countries which add to climate change will have a disproportionate impact on poorer parts of the world and create new risks and dangers for those in poverty in those countries. In the poorer parts of the world the cycle of poverty exacerbates the potential negative impacts of climate change. For those in poverty, weather-related disasters or a bad harvest can provide crippling economic shocks. Sometimes widespread famine and drought can affect entire nations. High levels of poverty and low levels of infrastructure development limit the capacity of poor communities to manage climate risks. With limited access to formal insurance, low incomes, and meagre assets, poor households have to deal with climate-related shocks under highly constrained conditions.[16]

So it turns out that caring for creation is not just about self-preservation or leaving a viable world for the next generation or preserving endangered species or habitats. These things are very important but are not the focus of this chapter. Our focus is to engage with the direct social justice dimension of caring for creation. This is about serving those in need—specifically in developing parts of the world.[17]

Taking the first steps

Many Christians believe, in general terms, that the care of creation is a good thing. More and more Christians are also becoming convinced about the significance of climate change. The recent coronavirus pandemic led to huge short-term drops in carbon emissions and air pollution in many parts of the world.[18] These welcome reductions could only be sustained if radical long-term lifestyle and policy changes are made. However, many Christians who understand these issues all too clearly may not have done much to address them and may be reluctant to have their consumerist lifestyles disturbed too much in the process. This is where the rubber hits the road! Those of us living in developed countries cannot address environmental issues without, at the same time, making significant changes to our lifestyles. This requires awareness and conviction—then action!

Here are some suggestions for taking the first steps on this journey.

The first aspect to consider is at a *personal and family lifestyle* level. I have shared already about some things my family has done. True change begins at home and in our small private worlds. That is where we need to begin. Some people may argue that such actions have minimal direct impact in the global context and are not worth bothering with. However, all change starts small and every person has to begin with themselves if they want to persuade others to follow them. It is also worth remembering that governments and retailers are keenly interested in consumer trends and tend to adopt policies which favour those trends.

The second aspect to consider is our *working lives*. There are many possible implications in the workplace and it can be quite challenging to influence workplace culture. The recent coronavirus pandemic has highlighted the creative possibilities of working from home for many types of employment.[19] However, we should use any possible opportunity to help shape the culture of our workplaces over such issues as recycling, use of water, waste management, transportation policies, and the issue of single-use plastics. Not many businesses have regular environmental audits—this needs to change. What happens in your place of work? Ask questions, make suggestions.

The third important aspect is *church life and culture*. When I first engaged with environmentalism, I initiated discussions in my church network and I ended up being asked to write a theological paper on the subject![20] It was an important moment for me because it firmed up my biblical convictions. The next step was that we had conversations in our local church management team about environmentally friendly changes we could adopt as a church community.

This process has been going on steadily for several years since then. We have made changes to our energy use and our focus on recycling. We have built a small garden and vegetable plot on our site, and we have encouraged the church members to embrace an environmentally aware lifestyle.

There are Christian organisations which can help us. In the UK there are a number of good examples such as Tearfund,[21] Climate Stewards,[22] A Rocha,[23] Operation Noah,[24] and Christian Climate Action.[25] A really helpful resource from A Rocha is the 'Eco Church' movement in which churches can undertake an audit and then register as 'Eco Churches'. This is a great way to bring about gradual practical change in churches.

The fourth aspect is to engage more strategically with *public policy*. We have recently entered a time in our national life where concern for the environment has become a significant issue for many people from all sorts of different political and social backgrounds. Major protest movements and pressure groups are growing in support and influence. Public policy really matters. Only governments and international agreements can bring about the amount of change in economic behaviour needed to truly address the huge environmental issues we face.

The best place to start is in your local community. Find out about the environmental policies of your local government or council. Talk to them about the issue. Make suggestions. Get involved. Then there is the wider national picture. In the UK, for example, important environmental issues come up regularly in national political debate and in the devolved governments of the UK. It takes a bit of effort to keep up with the issues, but organisations such as Tearfund can do much of the work for you. As a personal application, I began to talk to my MP about environmental issues a few years ago. This has been done regularly and face-to-face—and it has been a very positive dialogue.

Such is the general concern about environmental issues that we are seeing the new protest movements and pressure groups are likely to gain increasing influence. It is important to be well informed about these movements and consider carefully how, as Christians, we can be constructively involved.

The final aspect to consider is the potential for *partnerships with other community groups* involved in environmental issues. In the current social context there are often fantastic opportunities for building links in the local community and working together. Environmentalism is a key social concern for many who are outside the church. When we can work together, it will advance the cause and also provide an opportunity for sharing our faith. Here's an example. A friend of mine started a community garden in his city. Many people got involved. Most of them are not Christians. However, my friend has provided an opportunity for them to work together which they really appreciate. Many of them also ask him how his faith motivates him in this work!

Final reflection—an African story

This leads me to think again about my recent visit to Zambia. As I mentioned earlier, I am involved in a local church-based charity which is, among other things, sponsoring an exciting farming project in Zambia. We are helping churches in Zambia to teach and implement the 'Foundations for Farming' methodology in their communities.[26] This project originated in Zimbabwe and is designed to help smallholders in poorer countries to significantly increase their yields from key crops such as maize as well as from many fruits and vegetables. It has been remarkably successful. One key element in this methodology is 'zero tillage'. The land is not ploughed or dug up before planting. Rather, a suitable hole for each seed is dug in the soil. Seeds are planted carefully and individually. Why 'zero tillage'? Mainly because the root systems of existing plants help to retain moisture in the soil. This moisture retention is enhanced by the use of mulch or ground-covering plants. This is very significant in tropical countries where rainfall is limited or unpredictable. My friends in Zambia are excited about the potential for Foundations for Farming as it is gradually adopted in their communities. They are confident that it will help protect many people in African countries from the risk of desperate poverty due to food shortages. This is just one example of initiatives that are contributing to the fight against the negative impacts of climate change on the poorest.

Study Topics

This book is about lifestyle—developing a poverty-busting lifestyle. It is particularly about ensuring that our focus on specific issues of poverty in our community is matched by a lifestyle which demonstrates real poverty-busting intentions. Once we fully understand the social justice dimension of caring for creation, then we can engage practically with this vital issue.

1. Jesus' priority for his followers—loving our neighbours

Jesus made it clear that loving our neighbours is vital to discipleship—see Matthew 22:34–40. In the light of this, let's use the parable of the Good Samaritan as a basis for thinking about the issues raised in this chapter. Read Luke 10:25–37. Jesus is teaching about the practicalities of loving our neighbours. What is the main point that Jesus is making in this parable? How might we apply this point to the issues discussed in this chapter? Can people we do not know or may never meet be described as neighbours in a biblical sense? What implications does this have for us?

2. Thinking about our lifestyles

Our lifestyles are influenced by social pressures, advertising, social media, and the preferences of family or household members. We don't often take a step back and think about these influences. This is a great place to start when considering care for creation and its link to caring for those living in poverty.

In this chapter, I've given a few personal examples of lifestyle choices made by my family. They are not prescriptive; they are descriptive. It is just what we did. I deliberately did not give much detail. Details will vary a lot and are specific to each family or household and their differing situations. What matters is reflecting carefully on our lifestyles in the light of the specific conviction that our attempts to care for creation are important in caring for those in need.

Here are a few things to consider, either on your own, or, if you are able, with your family or household members.

- Discuss the main influences in your lifestyle choices relating to caring for creation.
- What new ideas have come to mind from reading this chapter?
- What practical steps can you take to build a poverty-busting lifestyle in this area?
- How can you become more informed and pro-actively involved in your local community and begin to influence policy and practice, locally and even nationally?

3. The church as an agent of change

Many readers will be members of local churches. If you are one of those people, then this section is for you!

Having reflected on personal lifestyles, the next step for us to think about is our faith community—our church. Local churches are ideal places to think about and act upon convictions about social justice issues. Some churches are engaged in environmental issues, others are not. Very few churches engage much with the direct social justice implications of environmentalism.

Here are a few questions to think about.

- What is your church already doing or discussing about this issue?
- Have you heard any biblical teaching on environmental issues in your church?

- What is the perspective of your minister or leadership team as far as you know?
- What opportunities do you have to engage your church in caring for creation—on behalf of those in poverty?
- Has your church engaged with any of the environmental pressure groups currently active?

CONCLUSION

Wherever we look in the Bible—Old Testament or New, Psalms or Proverbs, history or prophets, Gospels or Epistles—we see that God has always been deeply concerned about the plight of those facing poverty and injustice. Likewise, he has always called on those who worship him to care about those in need, as an active outworking of our devotion to him.

Isaiah calls it 'true fasting' and James calls it 'true religion'.[1] This is not an optional extra for Christians. Concerning ourselves with poverty and justice issues is an essential part of our relationship with our Father in heaven.

In some ways, it is relatively easy for us to agree with that and even to serve diligently at a church-run social action project while still maintaining a lifestyle that doesn't reflect God's heart for those in poverty. We can invest some of our time, energy, and money and still keep the needs of others at arm's length. In fact, sometimes giving just enough of what we have so that we feel we're doing our bit can be the method by which we allow ourselves to remain committed to our own comfort. I (Natalie) see that at work in my own heart sometimes: if I satisfy myself that I'm doing more than most, I let myself off the hook from living more radically and sacrificially.

In the process of writing together, Martin and I often discuss the balance between being measured and being provocative. Our aim in writing this book was to provide a challenge to all of us who care about poverty to ensure that our lives match up to what is in our hearts. That can be hard. We are on a journey. We dearly desire to be people who submit our whole lives to God—letting him have whatever he wants of our time, skills, energy, affections, and resources for his glory and for the good of those around us.

We have endeavoured to set out five specific challenges.

First of all, we recognise that it's possible to serve in our church social action projects but still have an unreformed lifestyle: we can inadvertently restrict our hearts for those in poverty to moments, or what is convenient to us, as well as separating our serving and giving in this area from our lives in general. We want to make sure that we live our lives in such a way as to tackle the poverty we see around us through our everyday actions and attitudes, not just when we set our minds to a specific project or act.

Secondly, we believe that poverty in various forms is accentuated if there is no place for particular types of people in our churches. There is still much work to be done to change the culture of church life and relationships to make church communities more accessible to people on the margins of society. The challenge is this: are the people we welcome to our projects also welcome into our lives? If there are people we would invite into the projects we run whom we would not invite into our lives in a meaningful, tangible sense, we have missed something of the heart of God and are potentially keeping at a distance the people God would have us get close to.

Thirdly, there is a call on us as individual Christ followers and as church families to move beyond treating the symptoms of poverty and injustice and towards addressing the root causes. This is much harder than simply helping people at their point of need, but is a crucial part of speaking up for the voiceless and bringing the justice of God to the people around us. Influencing the powerful may seem, to some, a more daunting task than helping the impoverished, but by doing so at a local and even national level, we have the opportunity to prevent others from being swept into poverty in the future. This is what it means to truly bring 'good news to the poor'[2] and to see the kingdom of God advance in our towns, cities, and villages. Your community should be blessed by the fact there are Christians in it.

Fourthly, as we begin to move beyond a personal and local focus, we see that our consumer habits can have far-reaching, even global, implications for people we may never meet or hear about. Nevertheless, if we are concerned about alleviating poverty, the impact of our small actions on people thousands of miles away should matter to us. How we live and particularly how we shop can make a difference to people locally and on the other side of the world. Rather than feel overwhelmed by this, what a wonderful opportunity to do good to others on a global scale.

This is also the case with our final study, which explored the impact we can have on the world around us in terms of environmental issues. Recognising that climate change is a pressing social justice concern should motivate us to think through how we operate as individuals, households, communities, and churches.

The global coronavirus pandemic threw each one of these challenges into sharper focus as this book went to print, making it all the more urgent for us to build poverty-busting lifestyles without delay.

We hope that *A Call to Act* will serve you well as a resource for making practical, intentional changes for the good of those in need around you, and for the good of those in need around the world.

ACKNOWLEDGEMENTS

A book like this is much more than the thoughts of two colleagues typed out on paper. There are so many conversations that take place behind the scenes, over months or years, shaping our thinking, challenging our ideas, pushing us to live radically. So there are many, many people to thank.

Special thanks are due, as always, to the other members of the Jubilee+ core team—our friends Pete and Sue Lyndon, Paul Mogford, and Andy Biggs—for your prayers, inspiration, insights, and encouragement at every step of the journey. Thanks, too, to two incredibly gifted women on our wider team: Sheena Gardner and Jennie Pollock.

Thank you to those who read the manuscript at an early stage and helped us to clarify our thoughts and put them across in more compelling ways—Phil Moore, John and Carol Evans, Alison Inglis-Jones, Karen Williams, Annmarie Moran, Sue Lyndon, Andy Biggs, Paul Mogford, Billie Anderson, Tim Nelson, and Paul Mann.

We are really grateful for the ongoing support, prayer, and advice of friends of Jubilee+ who keep us sharp! Thank you to

Angela and Greg Kemm, Ginny Burgin, Akhtar Shah, Jeremy and Ann Simpkins, Esther Swaffield-Bray, Sam Ward, and Nigel Ring.

It is a real pleasure to work with the outstanding team at David C Cook. Thank you for your commitment to this book and for letting us add in an extra chapter at the last minute! Thanks especially to Ian Matthews and Jack Campbell.

Martin thanks his church for supporting him in writing books. He is grateful to his fellow leaders and the members of Barnabas Community Church, Shrewsbury. This is the third time he's disappeared off into libraries and coffee shops for long periods to write!

Martin is also so grateful to his wife, Jane, and his family, who have been endlessly patient with his writing ideas and supplied him with encouragement and a listening ear along the way.

Natalie would like to thank the leadership team at King's Church in Hastings & Bexhill for their continued support and encouragement. Thanks also to the social action project leaders at King's—each one of you inspires me—and the whole church family.

Natalie is grateful to her faithful friends who patiently endure endless discussions about thoughts and ideas, and make her think more deeply: Joanna and Caner Mutu, Hannah Beaney, Kelly Ramshaw, Jon and Al Wales (and Isaac, Esther, Hudson, Poppy, and Moses), Liz Pursglove, Maddie Parsk, Sabiha Edwards, Santino and Emma Hamberis, Brian Marriott, Paul and Chloe Mann, Faye Thomson, Andrew Bunt, Deb Kurosu, Sarah Owen, Nick and Anna Heasman, Caelie Hawkins, Andrea Harwood, Dorothy Bourdet, Rachel Lewis, Hannah Latty, Liz Nevey, Alanna Reid, Claire Lockwood, Louise Cousins, Kate Thurston, Livy Gibbs, Michelle Earwaker, and Charlie Macdonald.

Thanks also to Jennie, Tamara, and Sheena for making my work-life so much easier. You bless me tremendously.

Extra special thanks from Natalie to Richard and Anna Wilson for deep conversations over so many lovely meals, for your constant support and care, for the story I love to tell, and for your encouragement—obviously! To Pete and Sue Lyndon for your great care for me. To Mark Evetts for trusting the process. To my coauthor who, despite all our jokes, is a real pleasure to write with. To Ezra, Ayla, and Izzy, who make my heart happy. And finally to Paula, Jonathan, and my legendary mum, Elaine.

NOTES

Introduction

1. Martin Charlesworth and Natalie Williams, *A Church for the Poor* (David C Cook, 2017), 40–46. Martin Charlesworth and Natalie Williams, *The Myth of the Undeserving Poor* (Grosvenor House, 2014), 68–69.

Chapter one: the abrupt call to act of the coronavirus pandemic

1. 'Novel Coronavirus (2019-nCoV) Situation Report—1', 21 January 2020, World Health Organisation, www.who.int/docs/default-source/coronaviruse /situation-reports/20200121-sitrep-1-2019-ncov.pdf.

2. Richard Partington, 'FTSE 100 posts largest quarterly fall since Black Monday aftermath', *The Guardian*, 31 March 2020, www.theguardian.com/business /2020/mar/31/ftse-100-posts-largest-quarterly-fall-since-black-monday-aftermath.

3. Phillip Inman, 'UK Covid-19 business bailouts have already cost more than £100bn', *The Guardian*, 30 April 2020, www.theguardian.com/world/2020 /apr/30/uk-coronavirus-business-bailouts-have-already-cost-more-than-100bn.

4. Neville Lazarus, 'Coronavirus: Millions in India facing hunger during COVID-19 lockdown measures', *Sky News*, 26 April 2020, https://news.sky.com/story /coronavirus-millions-of-indians-facing-hunger-during-covid-19-lockdown -measures-11978857.

5. Paul Anthem, 'Risk of hunger pandemic as COVID-19 set to almost double acute hunger by end of 2020', *Medium*, 16 April 2020, https://insight.wfp .org/covid-19-will-almost-double-people-in-acute-hunger-by-end-of-2020 -59df0c4a8072.

6. Michael Hirsh and Keith Johnson, 'A Tale of Two Rescue Plans', *Foreign Policy*, 24 April 2020, https://foreignpolicy.com/2020/04/24/united-states-europe -coronavirus-pandemic-shutdown-unemployment.

7. 'Coronavirus (COVID-19) roundup', Office for National Statistics, www.ons.gov.uk/peoplepopulationandcommunity/healthandsocialcare /conditionsanddiseases/articles/coronaviruscovid19roundup/2020-03- 26#deathsbyarea, accessed 4 May 2020; Dave Burke, 'Coronavirus: People in deprived areas twice as likely to die as North-South gap opens', *Mirror*, 1 May 2020, www.mirror.co.uk/news/uk-news/coronavirus-people-deprived- areas-twice-21952284; and 'Coronavirus: Higher death rate in poorer areas, ONS figures suggest', BBC News, 1 May 2020, www.bbc.co.uk/news/uk -52506979.

8. David Chipakupaku, 'Coronavirus: Woman "gang raped" in India while quarantined in school during lockdown', *Sky News*, 26 April 2020, https://news.sky.com/story/coronavirus-woman-gang-raped-in-india-while -quarantined-in-school-during-lockdown-11979103.

9. Amanda Taub, 'A New Covid-19 Crisis: Domestic Abuse Rises Worldwide,' *New York Times*, 6 April 2020, www.nytimes.com/2020/04/06/world/coronavirus -domestic-violence.html.

10. Information from IJM email, 'Prayer Partner Update #UnsafeinLockdown: 24th April 2020', https://mailchi.mp/91fb65b6b805/ijm-prayer-update-pray -for-6-children-now-free-662500?e=b13bf09a3f.

11. 'UK lockdown: Calls to domestic abuse helpline jump by half', BBC News, 27 April 2020, www.bbc.co.uk/news/uk-52433520.

12. Available at https://jubilee-plus.org/docs/A-Deepening-Crisis.pdf.

13. https://baby-basics.org.uk.

14. www.tlg.org.uk.

15. William Wan, 'The coronavirus pandemic is pushing America into a mental health crisis', *Washington Post*, 4 May 2020, www.washingtonpost.com/health /2020/05/04/mental-health-coronavirus/; 'Healthcare suicides: another tragic toll of the coronavirus pandemic', *New York Post*, 27 April 2020, https:// nypost.com/2020/04/27/health-care-suicides-another-tragic-toll-of

-coronavirus-pandemic/; Steve Sweeney, 'Nurse commits suicide in Italy due to trauma of working on frontline of coronavirus pandemic', *Morning Star*, 27 March 2020, https://morningstaronline.co.uk/article/w/nurse-commits-suicide-italy-due-trauma-working-frontline-coronavirus-pandemic.

16. 'Catching the virus: cybercrime, disinformation and the COVID-19 pandemic', Europol, 3 April 2020, www.europol.europa.eu/publications-documents/catching-virus-cybercrime-disinformation-and-covid-19-pandemic, 4, 7–9. 'Law enforcement in coronavirus online safety push as National Crime Agency reveals 300,000 in UK pose sexual threat to children', National Crime Agency, 4 April 2020, https://nationalcrimeagency.gov.uk/news/onlinesafetyathome. Jamie Grierson and Sally Weale, 'NCA predicts rise in online child sexual abuse during coronavirus pandemic', *The Guardian*, 2 April 2020, www.theguardian.com/society/2020/apr/03/nca-predicts-rise-in-online-child-sexual-abuse-during-coronavirus-pandemic#maincontent.

Chapter two: our context and our calling

1. 'Average actual weekly hours of work for full-time workers (seasonally adjusted)', Office for National Statistics, 13 August 2019. www.ons.gov.uk/employmentandlabourmarket/peopleinwork/earningsandworkinghours/timeseries/ybuy/lms. The legal maximum is an average of 48 hours per week.

2. 'How has life expectancy changed over time?', Office for National Statistics, 9 September 2015. www.ons.gov.uk/peoplepopulationandcommunity/birthsdeathsandmarriages/lifeexpectancies/articles/howhaslifeexpectancychangedovertime/2015-09-09.

3. 'National life tables, UK: 2016 to 2018', Office for National Statistics, 25 September 2019, www.ons.gov.uk/peoplepopulationandcommunity/birthsdeathsandmarriages/lifeexpectancies/bulletins/nationallifetablesunitedkingdom/2016to2018.

4. W. H. Auden, 'The Age of Anxiety', first published in the UK by Random House, 1948.

5. 'List of Countries by Projected GDP per capita', *Statistics Times*, 11 November 2019, http://statisticstimes.com/economy/countries-by-projected-gdp-capita.php.

6. It is also true that there are huge disparities of income between rich and poor in most developing countries, but this is not our major theme in this chapter.

The 'Gini Coefficient' is the method used to measure these disparities. See http://worldpopulationreview.com/countries/gini-coefficient-by-country/.

7. Patrick Butler, 'Report reveals scale of food bank use in the UK', *The Guardian*, 29 May 2017. www.theguardian.com/society/2017/may/29/report-reveals -scale-of-food-bank-use-in-the-uk-ifan.

8. Charlesworth and Williams, *Undeserving Poor*, 24–29, Charlesworth and Williams, *Church for the Poor*, 129–47.

9. 'Code on the Scheduling of Television Advertising', 1 April 2016. www.ofcom .org.uk/__data/assets/pdf_file/0014/32162/costa-april-2016.pdf.

10. 'Why TV remains the world's most effective advertising', thinkbox, 21 November 2017, www.thinkbox.tv/news-and-opinion/newsroom/why -tv-remains-the-worlds-most-effective-advertising/.

11. 'The Top 20 Valuable Facebook Statistics—Updated January 2020', Zephoria Digital Marketing, https://zephoria.com/top-15-valuable-facebook-statistics/.

12. World population stands at about 7.8 billion at the beginning of 2020. See www.worldometers.info/world-population/, accessed 13 January 2020.

13. 'Fact Check: how does social media affect your mental health?', *The Week,* 4 April 2019, www.theweek.co.uk/checked-out/90557/is-social-media -bad-for-your-mental-health.

14. Sabrina Barr, 'Six Ways Social Media Negatively Affects Your Mental Health', *The Independent*, 10 October 2019, www.independent.co.uk/life-style /health-and-families/social-media-mental-health-negative-effects-depression -anxiety-addiction-memory-a8307196.html; Laura Donnelly, 'Social media linked to increased risk of mental health problems', *The Telegraph*, 11 September 2019, www.telegraph.co.uk/news/2019/09/11/social -media-linked-increased-risk-mental-health-problems/.

15. Charlesworth and Williams, *Undeserving Poor*, 47.

16. See Matthew 3:13–17.

17. Charlesworth and Williams, *Undeserving Poor*, chapter 3; Charlesworth and Williams, *Church for the Poor*, chapter 3.

18. Matthew's gospel contains five major sections of discipleship teaching: Matthew 5:1–7:29; 10:1–11:1; 13:1–53; 18:1–19:1; 24:1–25; 26:1.

Chapter three: a life of simplicity

1. Harriet Constable, 'Your brand new returns end up in landfill', *BBC Earth*, www.bbcearth.com/blog/%3Farticle%3Dyour-brand-new-returns-end-up -in-landfill/, accessed 18 February 2020.

2. Matthew 6:33–34.

3. Matthew 6:19.

4. A well-respected resource in the UK is www.moneysavingexpert.com. See here for a review of current apps: www.thebalance.com/best-budgeting -apps-4159414.

5. DJS Research, 'Survey Highlights Loss of Neighbourly Spirit in UK', 28 November 2011, www.djsresearch.co.uk /PublicConsultationMarketResearchInsightsAndFindings/article /Survey-Highlights-Loss-of-Neighbourly-Spirit-in-UK-00239.

6. Monthly church attendance for over 16-year-olds in 2015. See Compassion UK, '6.02 million regular churchgoers in the UK', www.compassionuk.org /02-million-people-attending-church-regularly, accessed 28 August 2019.

7. Harriet Sherwood, 'British public turn to prayer as one in four tune in to religious services', *The Guardian*, 3 May 2020, www.theguardian.com /world/2020/may/03/british-public-turn-to-prayer-as-one-in-four-tune -in-to-religious-services.

8. See Acts chapters 2–7.

9. One of the key roles of Jubilee+ is to help churches to increase their capacity, as churches, to reach out to the vulnerable and marginalised in their local communities.

Chapter four: poverty-busting inclusivity

1. For the various measures of poverty used between 1968 and 2005, see Daniel Dorling et al., *Poverty, wealth and place in Britain, 1968 to 2005* (The Policy Press, 2007). Available online at www.jrf.org.uk/sites/default/files/jrf /migrated/files/2019-poverty-wealth-place.pdf.

2. Ben Lindsay, *We Need to Talk About Race* (SPCK, 2019), chapter 2.

3. Charlesworth and Williams, *Church for the Poor*, 124.

4. Ethnicity facts and figures, 'People living in deprived neighbourhoods', 16 March 2018. www.ethnicity-facts-figures.service.gov.uk/uk-population-by-ethnicity/demographics/people-living-in-deprived-neighbourhoods/latest.

5. 'Households Below Average Income, 2017/18, Children (detailed breakdowns)', Department for Work and Pensions, 28 March 2019, table 4.5db: Percentage of children in low-income groups by various family and household characteristics, United Kingdom (children-hbai-detailed-breakdown-2017 -18-tables.odb). Available at www.gov.uk/government/statistics/households -below-average-income-199495-to-201718.

6. 'BME workers far more likely to be trapped in insecure work, TUC analysis reveals', TUC, 12 April 2019. www.tuc.org.uk/news/bme-workers -far-more-likely-be-trapped-insecure-work-tuc-analysis-reveals.

7. Rianna Croxford, 'Coronavirus: Black African deaths three times higher than white Britons—study', BBC, 1 May 2020, www.bbc.co.uk/news /uk-52492662.

8. Charlesworth and Williams, *Church for the Poor*, chapters 10 and 11.

9. Charlesworth and Williams, *Church for the Poor*, chapter 9.

10. Ruth Perrin, '"They believed in me": The power of mentoring Millennials', Discipleship Research, May 2018. http://discipleshipresearch.com/2018/05 /they-believed-in-me-the-power-of-mentoring-millennials/.

11. Charlesworth and Williams, *Church for the Poor*, chapter 9.

Chapter five: changing your community

1. Multiple online sources, including www.theguardian.com/environment/2015 /dec/07/at-least-one-person-killed-in-floods-as-45000-homes-remain -without-power; www.timesandstar.co.uk/news/17025505.group-set -up-to-prepare-for-town-floods.

2. Vicky Foxcroft, 'Power the Fight: Tackling violence and the role of faith groups', 20 June 2019. www.vickyfoxcroft.org.uk/in-parliament/2019/06/20 /power-the-fight-tackling-violence-and-the-role-of-faith-groups.

3. www.graceadvocacy.org.

4. The Home Office is the UK government department that is responsible for the security, law, and order of the country.

Chapter six: buying for justice

1. Kaamil Ahmed, 'Coronavirus could turn back the clock 30 years on global poverty', *The Guardian*, 9 April 2020, www.theguardian.com/global-development/2020/apr/09/coronavirus-could-turn-back-the-clock-30-years-on-global-poverty.

2. Susanna Rustin, 'This cry for help on a Primark label can't be ignored', *The Guardian*, 25 June 2014, www.theguardian.com/commentisfree/2014/jun/25/primark-label-swansea-textile-industry-rana-plaza.

3. Cambodia is a good example. Its economy is heavily dependent on clothing manufacturing for export to richer countries. The EU is its biggest export market. Yet factory workers remain poorly paid and generally work in harsh working environments. The economic power remains with the richer countries buying clothes from Cambodia. See https://traid.org.uk/what-life-is-really-like-for-cambodian-garment-workers/.

4. A PDF of this data, downloaded from the Marks and Spencer interactive supply chain map for January 2020 can be viewed at http://j.mp/MandSClothing. View the map online at https://interactivemap.marksandspencer.com/.

5. A good way of doing this is to type into your search engine the name of the company you are investigating and then the words 'supply chain'.

6. Here, for example, is recent insight and research into working conditions in Amazon warehouses in the UK. Maya Wolfe-Robinson, 'Union stages final protest over "horrific" Amazon work practices', *The Guardian*, 22 July 2019, www.theguardian.com/technology/2019/jul/22/union-stages-final-protest-over-horrific-amazon-work-practices; 'Amazon: What's it like where you work?', Organise. Staff survey results available at http://j.mp/AmazonStaffSurvey17-18, accessed 14 February 2020. Other examples from similar companies in the UK are well documented.

7. See, for example, 'CLOSE THE GENDER PAY GAP', Fawcett Society, www.fawcettsociety.org.uk/close-gender-pay-gap, accessed 14 February 2020; Aleksandra Wisniewska et al., 'Gender Pay Gap: women still short-changed in the UK', *Financial Times*, 23 April 2019. https://ig.ft.com/gender-pay-gap-UK-2019/.

8. See, for example, Gwyn Topham, '£3.2bn UK pay gap for black, Asian and ethnic minority workers', *The Guardian*, 27 December 2018, www.theguardian.com/money/2018/dec/27/uk-black-and-ethnic-minorities-lose-32bn-a-year-in-pay-gap.

9. 'Zero hours contracts', *Economics Online*. www.economicsonline.co.uk /Labour_markets/Zero-hours-contracts.html, accessed 14 February 2020.

10. See, for example, 'Ban zero-hours contracts that exploit workers, says TUC', BBC News, 11 February 2019. www.bbc.co.uk/news/business-47193809.

11. For the story of Traidcraft, see Peter Johnson and Chris Sugden, ed., *Markets, Fair Trade and the Kingdom of God* (Regnum Books International, 2001).

12. Johnson and Sugden, *Markets, Fair Trade and the Kingdom*, 75.

13. 'The History of Traidcraft', www.traidcraft.co.uk/traidcraft-history, accessed 14 February 2020.

14. Note the Fairtrade Foundation vision and mission: 'We have a vision: a world in which all producers can enjoy secure and sustainable livelihoods, fulfil their potential and decide on their future. Our mission is to connect disadvantaged farmers and workers with consumers, promote fairer trading conditions and empower farmers and workers to combat poverty, strengthen their position and take more control over their lives', www.fairtrade.org.uk/What-is -Fairtrade/What-Fairtrade-does.

15. The six co-founders of Fairtrade Foundation were Oxfam, Traidcraft, Christian Aid, CAFOD, The World Development Movement, and New Consumer.

16. www.fairtrade.org.uk/Buying-Fairtrade, accessed 14 February 2020.

17. www.fairtrade.net/about/our-partners, accessed 14 February 2020.

18. www.christianaid.org.uk/campaigns, accessed 14 February 2020.

19. See: www.fairtrade.org.uk/get%20involved//In-your-community/Faith-Groups /Fairtrade-Churches, accessed 14 February 2020.

20. 'UK slavery network "had 400 victims"', BBC News, 5 July 2019. www.bbc.co .uk/news/uk-england-birmingham-48881327.

21. Adam Hewitt, 'Hope for Justice's key role in smashing of major modern slavery ring', Hope for Justice, 5 July 2019, https://hopeforjustice.org/news/2019 /07/hope-for-justices-key-role-in-smashing-of-major-modern-slavery-ring.

22. Other forms of modern slavery include forced child marriage, forced recruitment of child soldiers, forced criminality, and forced organ harvesting.

23. See 'Safe Car Wash', The Clewer Initiative, www.theclewerinitiative.org /safecarwash; and Alex Strangwayes-Booth, 'Safe Car Wash app reveals hundreds of potential slavery cases', BBC News, 7 April 2019, www.bbc .co.uk/news/uk-england-47829016.

24. www.ijm.org/slavery.

25. Thomas Lewis, 'Transatlantic slave trade', *Encyclopaedia Britannica*, 3 January 2020, www.britannica.com/topic/transatlantic-slave-trade.

26. For example, International Justice Mission, www.ijm.org; Hope for Justice, https://hopeforjustice.org; and Hope at Home, www.hopeathome.org.uk.

27. These campaigners also included freed black African slaves such as Olaudah Equiano, whose autobiography and campaigning activities had a major impact on the success of the movement.

28. See www.modernslaveryregistry.org or check the websites of individual retailers.

29. For example, www.slavefreealliance.org.

30. The Trussell Trust reports that in 2018 it had over four hundred foodbanks working from about 1,200 centres (www.trusselltrust.org/2018/11/27 /foodbanks-christmas-2018/). There are many independent foodbanks in operation as well.

31. 'WRAP restates UK food waste figures to support united global action', wrap.org.uk, 22 May 2018, www.wrap.org.uk/content/wrap-restates-uk -food-waste-figures-support-united-global-action. This figure includes the non-edible parts of the food waste. Edible food waste forms about 70 percent of this figure, or about five million tonnes.

32. 'Total number of households by region and country of the UK, 1996 to 2017', Office for National Statistics, 17 February 2016, updated 25 January 2018, www.ons.gov.uk/peoplepopulationandcommunity /birthsdeathsandmarriages/families/adhocs/005374 totalnumberofhouseholdsbyregionandcountryoftheuk1996to2015, accessed 21 August 2019.

33. For example, the various retail companies in the wider Co-operative Group. See www.co-operative.coop.

34. A good place to start is to access information from www.fairtrade.org.uk. There are also some sector-specific sources of information such as https://knowtheorigin.com which deals with fairtrade and organic fashion.

Chapter seven: care for creation

1. See www.climatestewards.org.

2. Some Christians have sought to avoid the force of this Genesis truth by focusing primarily on biblical descriptions of final judgement which involve both

humanity and the natural world. However, this fails to take account of the prophetic significance of our care of creation now and its ultimate fulfilment in the emergence of a 'new heaven and a new earth' (Revelation 21–22).

3. 'Child Survival Fact Sheet: Water and Sanitation', UNICEF, 4 June 2004, www.unicef.org/media/media_21423.html.

4. www.wateraid.org/facts-and-statistics, accessed 14 February 2020.

5. WHO estimates that every year 4.2 million people die due to outside air pollution and 3.8 million die from indoor air pollution from fuels and smoke. See www.who.int/airpollution/en/.

6. Mari Williams et al., *No time to waste: Tackling the plastic pollution crisis before it's too late* (Tearfund, 2019), 13, https://learn.tearfund.org/~/media/files/tilz /circular_economy/2019-tearfund-consortium-no-time-to-waste-en.pdf?la=en.

7. For a helpful scientific and biblical perspective on the significance of the marine environment, see Dr Robert Sluka, 'Hope for the Ocean: Marine Conservation, Poverty Alleviation and Blessing the Nations', Grove Booklet, E 165, 2012.

8. 'We did it! Microbeads Ban Comes Into Effect', Greenpeace, 11 January 2018, www.greenpeace.org.uk/news/we-did-it-microbeads-ban-comes-into-effect.

9. Laura Parker, 'Here's how much plastic trash is littering the earth', www.nationalgeographic.com/news/2017/07/plastic-produced -recycling-waste-ocean-trash-debris-environment/.

10. www.foundationsforfarming.org.

11. www.ipcc.ch.

12. According to a World Metrological Organization (WMO) report published in 2019, atmospheric concentrations of carbon dioxide and other greenhouse gases reached new highs in 2018. Since 1990 there has been an increase of 43 percent in the warming effect on the climate of long-lived greenhouse gases. Using data from monitoring stations in the Arctic and all over the world, researchers say that in 2018 concentrations of CO_2 reached 407.8 parts per million (ppm), up from 405.5 ppm a year previously. This increase was above the average for the last ten years and is 147 percent of the 'pre-industrial' level in 1750. The WMO also records concentrations of other warming gases, including methane and nitrous oxide. About 40 percent of the methane emitted into the air comes from natural sources, such as wetlands, with 60 percent from human activities, including cattle farming, rice cultivation, and landfill dumps. Methane is now at 259 percent of the pre-industrial level, and the increase seen over the past year was higher than

both the previous annual rate and the average over the past ten years. Nitrous oxide is emitted from natural and human sources, including from the oceans and from fertiliser-use in farming. According to the WMO, it is now at 123 percent of the levels that existed in 1750. What concerns scientists is the overall warming impact of all these increasing concentrations. Known as total radiative forcing, this effect has increased by 43 percent since 1990 and is not showing any indication of stopping. See https://public.wmo.int/en/media/press-release/2019-concludes-decade-of-exceptional-global-heat-and-high-impact-weather.

13. It is beyond the scope of this chapter to refer to the many other important dimensions of environmentalism and climate science.

14. There are, of course, many other environmental issues of great concern, such as loss of bio-diversity, specific areas of pollution, the long-term loss of ice in the polar regions, the advance of deserts, rising sea levels, etc. These are not our main focus in this context.

15. For example, John Houghton, *Global Warming* (Cambridge University Press, 2015), 145.

16. We should also note that climate change also has negative impacts on the poorer parts of UK society. See Ian Preston et al., 'Climate change and social justice: An evidence review', Joseph Rowntree Foundation, February 2014, www.jrf.org.uk/sites/default/files/jrf/migrated/files/climate-change-social-justice-full.pdf.

17. It is also true that the over-consumption, pollution, and increasing carbon footprint of richer sectors in developing countries have an adverse effect on the poor in their own nations. This is an important issue and needs to be addressed—but is not the focus of this chapter because our intended primary readership is in the developed world.

18. 'Carbon emissions are falling sharply due to coronavirus. But not for long', *National Geographic*, 6 April 2020, www.nationalgeographic.co.uk/environment-and-conservation/2020/04/carbon-emissions-are-falling-sharply-due-coronavirus-not-long.

19. Zoe Kleinman, 'How will coronavirus change the way we live?', BBC, 30 April 2020, www.bbc.co.uk/news/explainers-52356136.

20. Martin Charlesworth, 'Towards a Christian Approach to the Environment', July 2010. Available at https://jubilee-plus.org/reports/3/towards-a-christian-approach-to-the-environment/.

21. www.tearfund.org.

22. www.climatestewards.org.

23. https://arocha.org.uk/.

24. https://operationnoah.org/.

25. https://christianclimateaction.org/. See Christian Climate Action, *Time to Act* (SPCK, 2020), for an important discussion of Christian engagement with political climate action movements such as Extinction Rebellion.

26. www.foundationsforfarming.org.

Conclusion

1. Isaiah 58; James 1–2.

2. Isaiah 61:1; Luke 4:18.

ABOUT THE AUTHORS

Martin Charlesworth

Martin lives in Shrewsbury with his wife, Jane, and has three grown-up daughters. He holds degrees in history and theology, and worked as a teacher and in business before becoming a church leader. Martin led Barnabas Community Church, Shrewsbury, from 1994 to 2014 and helped develop its strong emphasis on social action and community engagement.

In his spare time, Martin enjoys cycling, squash, and mountaineering. He is an enthusiastic traveller, having previously lived in Pakistan and South Africa.

Martin leads Jubilee+.

Natalie Williams

Natalie grew up in a working-class family in Hastings, one of the most deprived areas of Britain. She was the first person in her family to go to university. After graduating, she worked as a journalist in London and Beijing. She has an MA in Political Communications.

Natalie is currently Head of Communications & Policy at Jubilee+ and Community Engagement Director at King's Church in Hastings & Bexhill, where she oversees social action.

She is passionate about Christians and churches being a force for good in their communities and actively demonstrating the mercy of God to those in need.

ABOUT JUBILEE+

Jubilee+ is a UK charity that equips churches of all denominations to be increasingly effective at serving and supporting those who are vulnerable or trapped in poverty in our communities. Our vision is to see the church in the UK be a champion of those in hardship and a means to healthy communities across the nation.

This is a big vision. It's based on the fact that we believe we serve a big God, whose heart is especially inclined towards those in poverty. We also believe that his church has a responsibility not only to care for and empower those in need but also to speak up on behalf of the voiceless.

Our vision goes beyond seeing individual lives transformed—as important as that is—to seeing entire neighbourhoods and communities strengthened so that our society as a whole is healthier. Our conviction is that when churches are at the heart of social action, social justice, and social enterprise, society flourishes.

A Call to Act is the third book written by the Jubilee+ team, following *The Myth of the Undeserving Poor* (2014, Grosvenor House) and *A Church for the Poor* (2017, David C Cook).

Find us at: www.jubilee-plus.org
Twitter, Facebook, and Instagram: @jubileeplus

Small group resources from David C Cook

Mission Shaped Living

More than just a tool box of 'how to do evangelism,' over eight sessions Mission Shaped Living will build spiritual practices, vision, hope, and confidence into your life so that sharing God's love with others becomes a joy and not a burden.

LEADER'S GUIDE: £8.99
ISBN: 9780830781812

PARTICIPANT'S GUIDE: £9.99
ISBN: 9780830781805

Visit www.missionshapedliving.co.uk for bulk purchase offers and more information

Saints Alive!

Saints Alive! is a well-loved nine-week course introducing people to faith in God through the power of the Holy Spirit, helping them to be integrated into the life of the church and moving out into ministry in their everyday lives. Fully revised for the 21st century, and with a leader's manual, optional videos, and a journal for every member that includes teaching, Bible readings, and space to record thoughts, *Saints Alive!* has been used by hundreds of thousands all over the world—and with this new and updated edition it will be used more widely still.

Visit www.saintsalive.co.uk for pre-order offers and more information

LEADER'S MANUAL: £8.99
ISBN: 9780830781485

PARTICIPANT'S JOURNAL: £9.99
ISBN: 9780830781492

DVD: £14.99
ISBN: 9780830781508

DAVID C COOK
transforming lives together